Basic
QUILTING

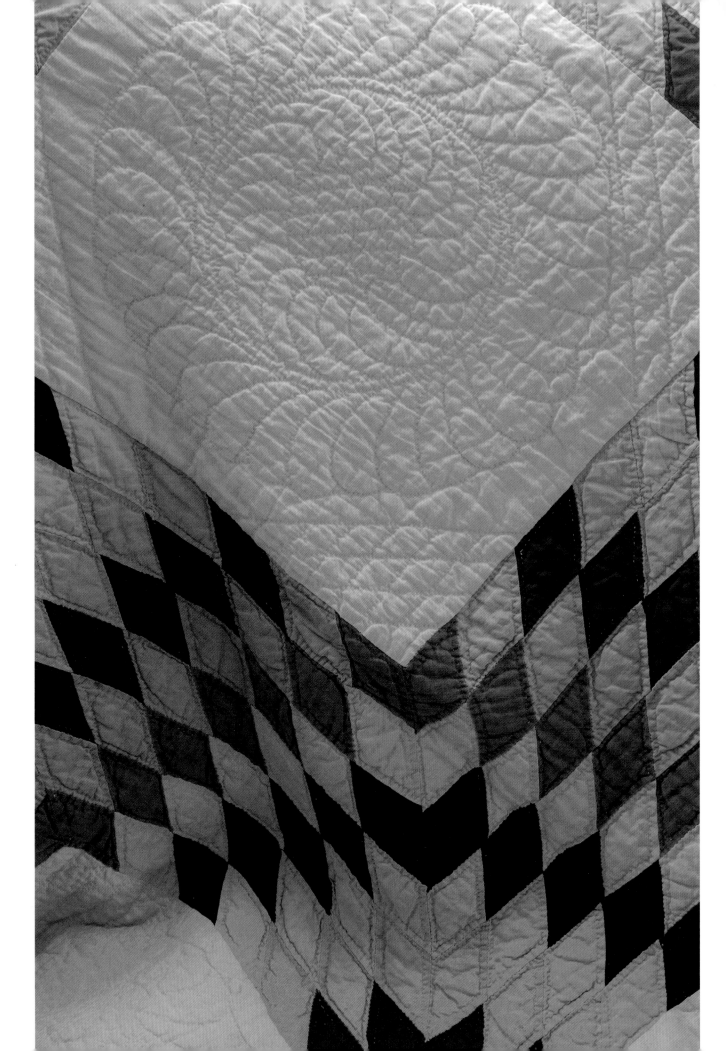

Basic QUILTING

All the Skills and Tools You Need to Get Started

Sherrye Landrum, *editor*

Charlene Atkinson,
expert quilter and consultant

Photographs by
Alan Wycheck

STACKPOLE
BOOKS

Copyright © 2007 by Stackpole Books

Published by
STACKPOLE BOOKS
5067 Ritter Road
Mechanicsburg, PA 17055
www.stackpolebooks.com

Printed in China

First edition

10 9 8 7 6 5 4 3 2 1

Cover design by Tracy Patterson
Cover photographs by Alan Wycheck

Library of Congress Cataloging-in-Publication Data

Basic quilting : all the skills and tools you need to get
started / Sherrye Landrum, editor ; Charlene Atkinson,
expert quilter and consultant ; photographs by Alan Wycheck.
     p. cm.
   Includes bibliographical references.
   ISBN-13: 978-0-8117-3348-9 (hidden spiral bound pb)
   ISBN-10: 0-8117-3348-3 (hidden spiral bound pb)
 1. Quilting. 2. Patchwork. I. Landrum, Sherrye.
II. Atkinson, Charlene.

TT835.B2757 2007
747.46'041—dc22

2006010739

Contents

Acknowledgments

I now realize that the beautiful quilt you see in someone's home or in a photograph in a magazine is just the tip of the iceberg of the wide and wonderful world of quilting. For welcoming me to quilting and showing me the way, I thank, first and foremost, Charlene Atkinson, who is the most enthusiastic, organized, and talented partner an author could ever hope to find! Her antiques and table-setting expertise benefited this book as well. I thank the other ladies in the Tuesday morning quilt group: Jeanie Weddle, Donna Nagle, Chris Higbee, and Chris Nerheim, who donated quilts, advice, time, and encouragement to this project. I appreciate Janet Shultzabarger of Calico Corners in Carlisle, Pennsylvania, for allowing me to ask so many questions. My hat is off to Cathy Queitzsch, owner of Smile Spinners in Marysville, Pennsylvania, for providing her bright and welcoming store so we could photograph all the materials a quilter needs. I thank Alan Wycheck of Wycheck Photography in Harrisburg, Pennsylvania, for his cheerful magic with a camera and for helping this book come into being.

Introduction

The fact is that humans like to make things—things that are useful, things that are beautiful. Quilts are both. In this book you will find the information and instructions that you need to sew and quilt by hand. These beginning projects are smaller than a bread basket, so they won't take long, but the skills are the same ones you would use to make a king-sized quilt! If you begin with the first project, you will add skills and gain experience as you go through the book.

The first thing I learned about quilting is its "democratic" nature. While there are thousands of expert quilters, there are no rules. You are free to make quilts any way you like. When you pick up a needle and pieces of fabric, you are following in the footsteps of many generations of women (and men) before you. They sewed quilts first out of necessity, using whole cloth if they had it, and then cutting pieces out of leftover fabric or worn-out clothes. Nothing was wasted. But the quilters of the past, especially during the 1800s, went beyond usefulness to develop striking patterns for their quilts—creating works of art that are truly American in their inventiveness and variety.

What Makes Up a Quilt?

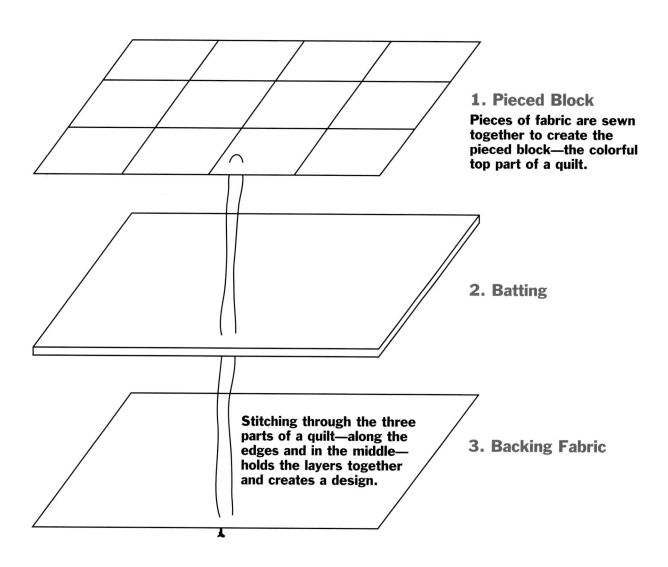

1. Pieced Block
Pieces of fabric are sewn together to create the pieced block—the colorful top part of a quilt.

2. Batting

Stitching through the three parts of a quilt—along the edges and in the middle—holds the layers together and creates a design.

3. Backing Fabric

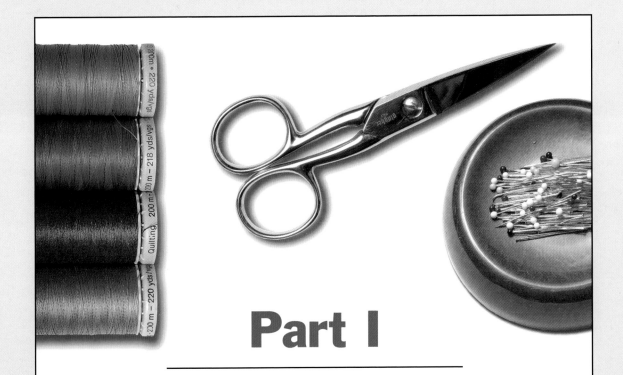

Part I

Supplies and Beginning Steps

1

Quilting Materials and Equipment

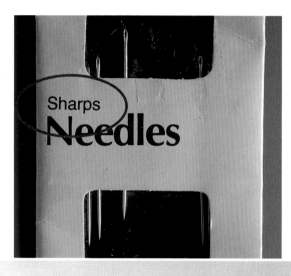

NEEDLES

Most people would agree that the first tool of quilting was and still is a needle. But you'll need more than one. Sharps are used for general sewing. A size 10 sharp needle will do fine for hand-piecing projects in this book. "Betweens" are the needles used for quilting. Beginners may want to start quilting with a size 10 between needle. It's important to know that the higher the number on the needle, the smaller and thinner it is. Experienced quilters like short needles to make short stitches, but you should start with a needle that fits your hand and is comfortable to use. Sharps and betweens come in packages of assorted sizes, so you can experiment to find the ones that work best for you. You'll need some extras as the needle you sew with will become dull over time.

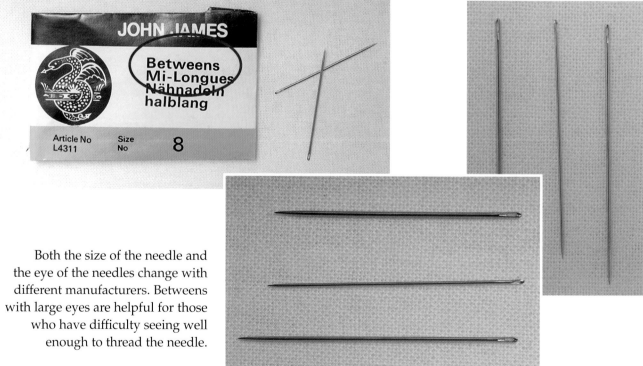

Both the size of the needle and the eye of the needles change with different manufacturers. Betweens with large eyes are helpful for those who have difficulty seeing well enough to thread the needle.

SELF-THREADING NEEDLES AND NEEDLE THREADERS

Some people can't get the thread to go through the eye of the needle. Try wetting the end of the thread so it doesn't fray. Cut the thread after you have tried a couple of times; many times a fresh cut will work. Or try threading the other side of the eye of the needle. If you still can't get it threaded, you might want to use a self-threading needle or a needle threader.

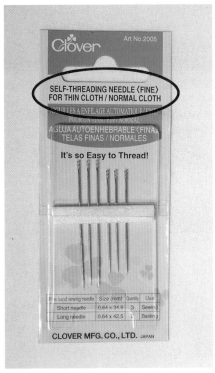

Self-Threading Needles

The eyes of these needles are larger, so it may snag on the fabric as you pull it through several layers.

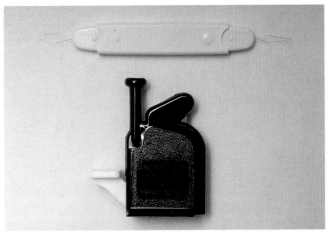

Needle Threaders

The one on the top is a simple wire that goes through the eye of the needle. The one pictured on the bottom is more complicated but just as effective at threading the needle.

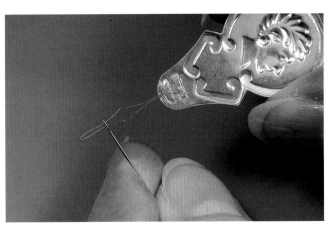

To use the wire type of needle threader: Insert the point of the thin wire into the eye of the needle.

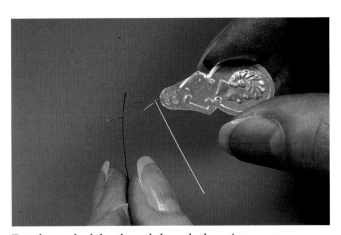

Put the end of the thread though the wire.

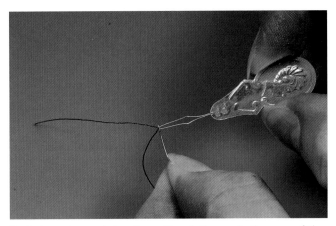

Pull the wire and the thread back through the eye of the needle.

THREAD

Use 100 percent cotton thread for piecing and quilting. Thread with polyester in it will stretch and won't look smooth when the quilt is finished. Cotton thread does not knot as easily either.

Quilting thread is thicker than the thread used for piecing, and it has a waxy coating. If you cannot find the color of quilting thread that you want, you can buy regular thread and coat it yourself with beeswax. Pull the thread across the surface of a square of beeswax to put on the waxy coating.

Quilting stitches made with dark thread on light fabrics will be more visible than stitches done with light-colored thread.

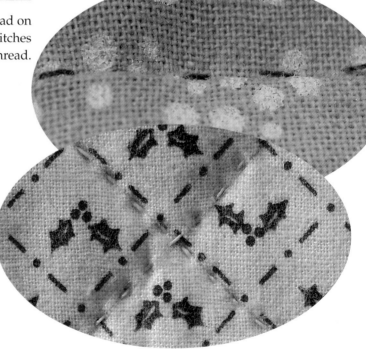

If you often get knots where you don't want them, you might try a special type of wax to coat the thread so it will go through fabric more smoothly and prevent some of the knots. Pull the thread across the surface of the wax to coat it. Also, try sewing with a shorter length of thread. If it's too long, it will tangle more easily.

4

SCISSORS

It's best to have a pair of scissors that you use only for cutting fabric and thread. Cutting paper with fabric scissors will dull them. You need to make nice clean cuts in the fabric with no ragged edges or pulled threads. There are many styles and sizes of scissors to choose from. Pinking shears have grooved blades and make a distinctive V cut in the fabric that helps keep it from unraveling.

The handles of fabric scissors are angled so that it is easier to cut fabric on a flat surface.

You can also cut fabric with scissors like these.

These are small embroidery scissors you can carry with you to cut threads. They don't work well for cutting large pieces of fabric.

If you don't want to carry scissors with you—or can't because you're going on an airline—you might invest in a thread cutter that looks like a piece of jewelry. Each of the grooves in the circle can cut thread.

5

ROTARY CUTTER AND BOARD

You may also cut fabric with a rotary cutter and the special board that is to be used along with it to prevent damage to the work surface under the fabric. These blades are very sharp. Please be careful when you are using one. *Always* put the blade cover up after you cut the fabric. This can be simply done, usually with a push of a button.

A rotary cutter and board cost more than a pair of scissors, but they help you make very accurate cuts in the fabric. You won't need to purchase a rotary cutter for the projects in this book, but if you intend to quilt larger projects, you might want to invest in one.

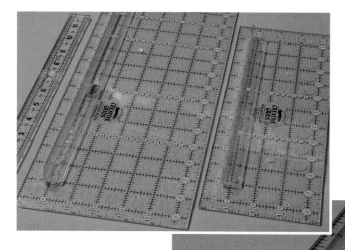

RULER

You will need a clear ruler (so you can see the fabric underneath) for drawing sewing lines and cutting out templates. Purchase a good one to be sure that the measurements are accurate! If you compare different rulers at the store by putting them side by side, you can see that some are off by as much as $1/4$ inch or more. When you piece and quilt, your seams are only $1/4$ inch wide. If your ruler is incorrect, you might be surprised at the final size of your project—and perhaps frustrated that the design doesn't come out right.

There are many sizes of rulers. The larger ones have printed grids to help you measure before you cut the fabric.

If you use a rotary cutter, you can buy a guard to put on the ruler to protect your fingers from the blade. When you are cutting, one hand holds the ruler on the fabric, and the other hand rolls the cutter down the edge of the ruler, making a perfect cut. The guard protects the hand that is holding the fabric steady.

SEAM RIPPER

Sometimes stitches are not as smooth, straight, or small as we would like. Or you may have gotten a knot in your thread or the thread broke, and you need to start over. A seam ripper can help you remove stitches quickly. Use a good light to work under, so you can see the stitches clearly. Take your time, so you will not snag the fabric. If you pull a thread that is part of the fabric, you may ruin the piece and have to cut a new one. Ripping out goes more quickly if you cut every third stitch and then pull the thread out.

THIMBLES

You will need a thimble or something to protect your fingers from the sharp point of the needle. It's an occupational hazard of hand-sewing, and experts need thimbles just as much as beginners. You'll develop a callus on the finger that's below the fabric when you're quilting, but a thimble is your friend. Most of us have seen a traditional metal thimble, but there are a wide variety of materials and types of thimbles on the market. Some may fit your fingers better than others. Here are a leather one with a metal disc in the tip, a metal one, and a band made of leather and plastic.

There are thimble pads made of leather with a sticky backing, so you can stick them on your finger to protect it from the needle's point. Place these pads wherever you need them. They are easier to wear than a regular thimble, which can get uncomfortable or hot.

If you have long fingernails, you may want a thimble with an open top or a band thimble. As you sew, you may find that you push the eye of the needle with the side of the thimble, not with the end of it. Remember, there are no rules. Do whatever is comfortable for you.

PATTERNS OR TEMPLATES

You will need a template for each of the pieces in your quilt block. You use templates to cut the fabric pieces that go in the quilt block. The plastic sheets made for templates are thin but sturdy, last longer than cardboard, and don't lose shape like cardboard does. Template plastic has a grid printed on it to help you cut out the proper size of pattern easily and quickly.

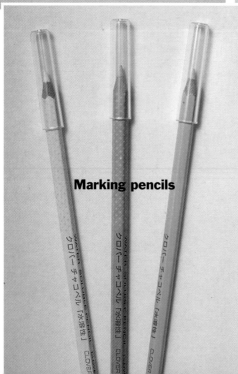

Tailor's chalk

PENCILS OR FABRIC MARKERS

You may use mechanical pencils with fine lead or other marking tools to mark seam lines and quilting lines on your fabric. Press lightly. It is important that the marks wash out when you are finished quilting. That's why you don't use a ballpoint or felt-tip pen. Even marking pens that have water-soluble ink can cause problems if the heat of the iron sets the ink in the fabric. Read the manufacturer's directions on any marking pens or pencils. Tailor's chalk has been used for centuries to mark lines on fabric, but it wipes off easily and may be gone before you're finished stitching along it. Liquid chalk is another type of marker.

Liquid chalk

Marking pencils

Marking pens

BRASS SAFETY PINS

Brass safety pins are used for holding the three layers of the quilt together. Brass is the best material because it doesn't rust, which comes in handy if the quilt project gets wet or takes a long time to complete.

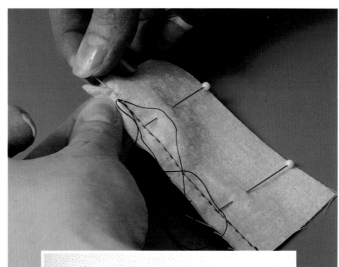

LONG QUILTING PINS, SILK PINS

There are different sizes of pins, just as there are different sizes of needles. Quilt pins are longer than regular pins, so they can hold all the layers of fabric together. These pins often have colored glass balls or fabric tops so you can see them in the fabric— and if you drop them on the carpet. You will need pins to hold pieces of fabric together until you sew the seam. Remove the pins as you sew, and put them in a pin box or pin cushion.

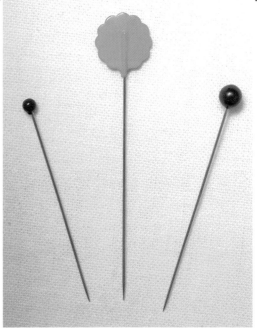

PIN CUSHION

It's important to keep your pins together safely, so you don't end up stepping on them. The one in the picture is magnetized so the pins can't fall out. In the common red "tomato" style pin cushion, the little strawberry on top is an emery bag. You can sharpen your needles and pins by sticking them into the bag several times.

9

IRON

You will need to use a steam iron for pressing the seams. This is very important for the appearance of the finished project, but you'll also be pressing seams as you sew them. Use the permanent press setting, so you won't scorch the fabric. Press the seam onto the darker fabric so it won't show through the light fabric when you look at it from the front.

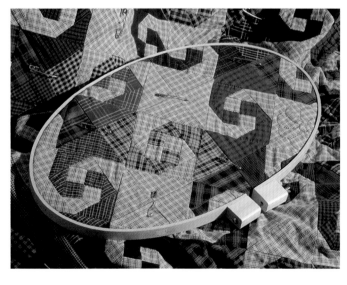

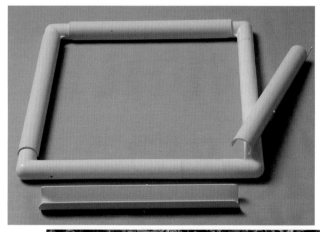

QUILTING HOOP OR FRAME

If you have a large project to quilt, you might want to get a quilting hoop or frame to hold the fabric while you stitch. Frames come in many different sizes, ranging from small portable hoops and squares to standing frames that sit on the floor by your chair and hold the quilt. There are even quilt frames that hold a bed-sized quilt so many quilters can work together. For the projects in this book, you don't need a frame.

FABRIC

The best fabric to use for your quilt is 100 percent cotton. It should be machine washable and shouldn't unravel easily. Check the cut edge and make sure there are not a lot of threads hanging loose. You also don't want it too thick, such as a denim or canvas fabric. When you walk into a fabric store, you may feel overwhelmed at first and wonder how you will be able to choose just a few fabrics from so many. Many stores group cottons that are suitable for quilts together.

Several of the projects in this book use "fat quarters," which are ½-yard pieces of fabric cut down the middle, so the size of each piece is 18 x 22 inches (45 x 56 cm). Many fabric stores have fat quarters and fat eighths already packaged in rolls of coordinating colors to simplify your first fabric choices.

Fabric on bolts comes in various widths. It may be 22 inches wide, 44/45 inches wide, or 60 inches wide. If you're not sure how wide it is, ask before you have it cut.

BATTING

Batting is the cushioning layer between the quilt top and the backing. It provides warmth and gives definition to the quilting stitches. Batting comes in different thicknesses. For the projects in this book, you'll want to have thin- or medium-weight batting. The thicker the batting is, the more difficult it is to stitch through.

There are many types of batting: Cotton, cotton/polyester, polyester, silk, and wool. Cotton or cotton/polyester blends are recommended for the projects in this book. You might buy a package of batting, or you can have it cut off of a large roll of batting just as you do with fabric. Read the instructions on the package, because you may need to wash the batting before using it. Unroll it and smooth out the folds. Some battings work better for hand quilting than others. Not too puffy!

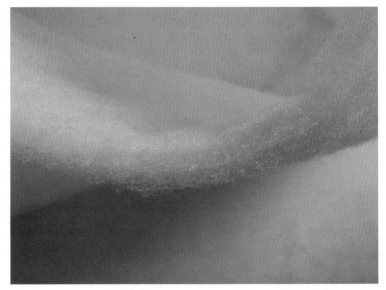

This batting is too fluffy for our projects. It is better for a tied quilt (see page 67).

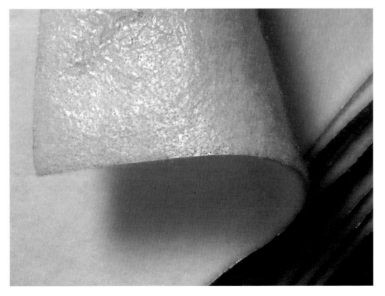

You can buy batting that has been treated to resist heat to use in hot pads, like the one in this book. The shiny side is the heat-protective coating.

2

Basic Knots and Stitches

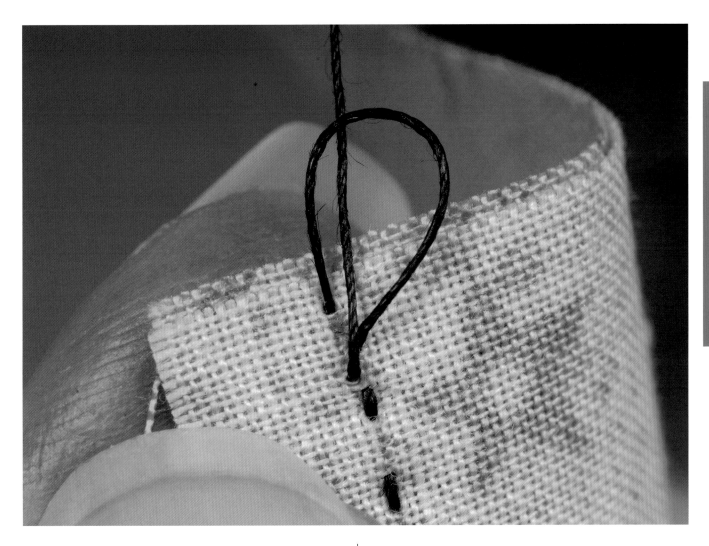

If you have never done any needlework, be sure to practice your stitching so you can develop the skills that make quilting fun. The stitches are simple. You will master them quickly—and you may surprise yourself by preferring to use one hand instead of the other.

Use good quality thread. Cheap thread frays and breaks easily. Generally good quality thread will not be found in the three spools for $1 bin. Ask the fabric store salesperson for help finding good quality thread. Start with neutral or light colors that blend in with the fabrics

in the quilt, and your stitches won't stand out so much. Try starting with an 18- to 20-inch length of thread. If it's any longer, it may tangle and make a knot where you don't want one.

Try not to let the thread twist. You may have to hold the fabric up and let the threaded needle dangle below to untwist the thread. Or you can slide the eye of the needle all the way down to where the thread is coming out of the fabric. As you slide the needle eye back up the thread, it should untwist.

Quilter's Knot

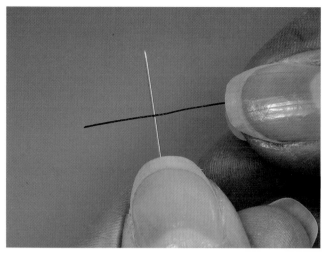

1. To make a knot at the end of the thread before you start stitching, thread the needle.

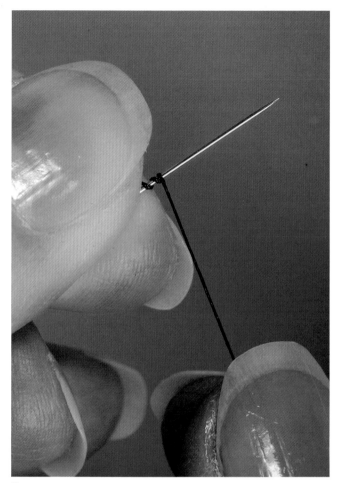

3. Keep the loops close together on the needle and pull on the thread to make sure the loops are tightly wrapped around the needle.

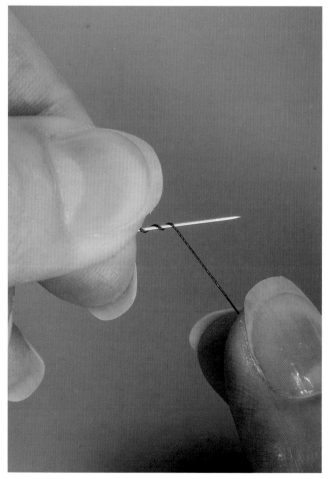

2. Hold the end of the thread against the needle with one hand and wrap the thread three times around the needle.

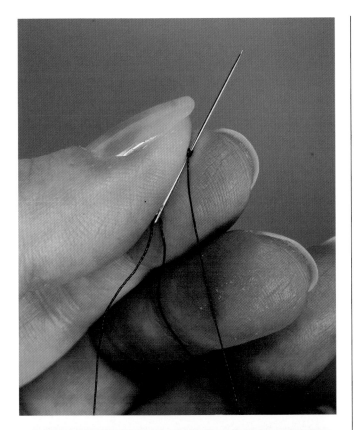

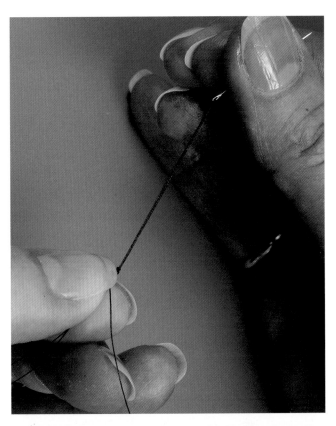

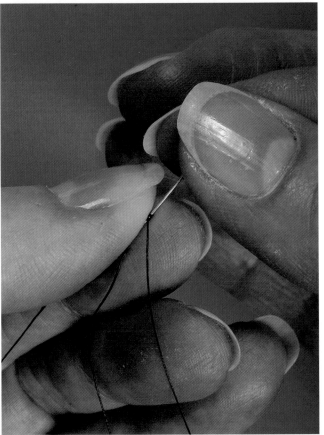

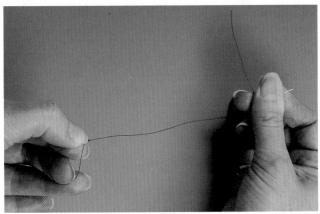

5. Keep pinching the loops as you slide them down the thread to the end. The loops will roll over each other and create the knot.

4. Pinch the loops against the needle and gently pull the needle through the loops. Keep your thumb and finger pressed together all the way to the end of the thread.

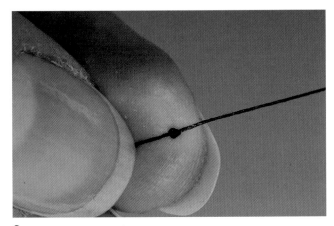

6. Pull the knot tight.

15

The Knot at the Beginning of Quilting

The knot should be buried in the layer of batting, so it can't be seen on either side of the quilt.

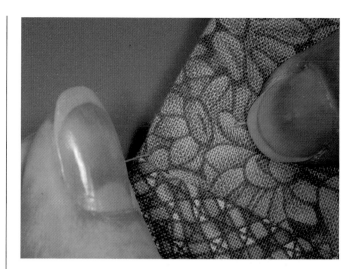

Insert the needle about an inch away from where you will start quilting. Only go through the quilt top and the batting, don't catch the backing fabric.

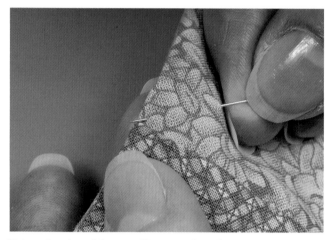

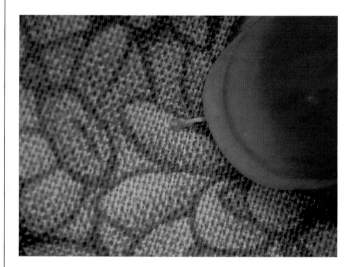

Bring the tip of the needle up right where you want to begin. (In this example, the needle comes up right beside the seam line to do "stitch in the ditch" quilting.)

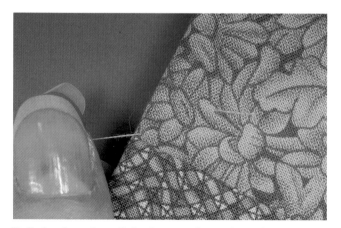

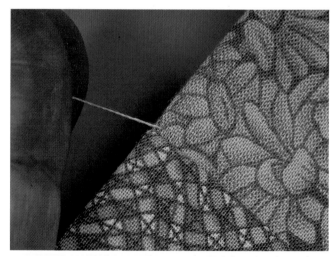

Press on the knot with your thumbnail and keep pulling on the thread until the knot pops through the fabric—and stays in the batting layer.

Pull the thread until the knot at the end touches the fabric.

The Knot at the End of Quilting

When you're about to run out of thread or you have finished quilting a row, you need to make a knot in the quilting thread and bury it inside the batting so it can't be seen. Practice a bit and this will become second nature to you.

Put the needle next to the thread where it comes up through the fabric. This is right at the last stitch you've made.

Hold the needle close to the fabric.

Wrap the thread three times around the point of the needle.

Keep the loops snug on the needle by pulling gently on the thread. Insert the tip of the needle into the top and batting only. Do not catch the backing.

Bring the needle tip out of the fabric about ½ inch away from where it went in. Don't worry; there will not be a stitch there. It will not show when the knot is done.

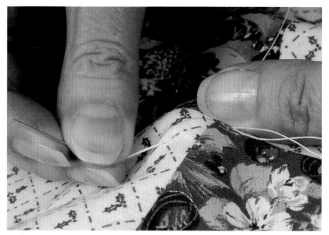

Hold the loops tightly in place on the fabric as you pull the thread through them. Keep holding until you reach the end of the thread.

Pull the knot tight. While this knot is small, you don't want it to show. You will encourage it to slip between the threads of the fabric and disappear into the middle batting layer of the quilt.

Once the knot is hidden, pull on the thread just a little more, and clip it close to the fabric. Lay the scissors flat against the quilt top so you cut only the thread.

Press down on the knot firmly with your thumbnail. You can bury the knot in the batting layer by tugging gently on the thread until the knot slips through the quilt top fabric. Smooth the fabric with one hand to balance the tension on the knot coming from the thread in your other hand. Easy does it.

Smooth out the fabric, and the end of the thread disappears. If there is still a bit of thread showing, pull on it while bunching up the fabric a little to allow you to see more of the thread. Cut it again and when you smooth the quilt out flat, the thread should not show. Be careful not to tug on the thread so much that you pull the knot through, too! You should not see the knot.

Backstitch Loop Knot

Use this knot at the beginning and end of a seam. You can also make backstitch loops at several places along the seam to strengthen it. Begin by taking a stitch at the edge of the fabric on the seam line.

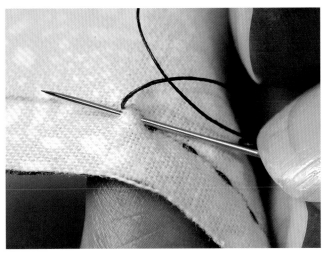

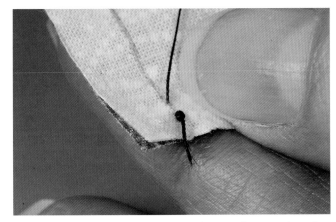

Pull the thread taut, and then make another stitch right on top of the first one.

You sew the seam with a running stitch, which is demonstrated on the next page. At the end of the seam, make another backstitch loop. Do not pull the thread all the way through this time. Leave a loop in the thread instead. Put the point of the needle through the loop.

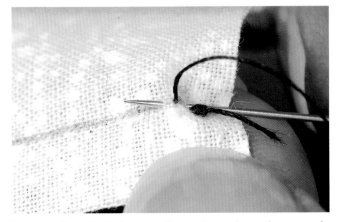

Pull the thread all the way through, and you have made a backstitch loop to anchor the beginning of the seam.

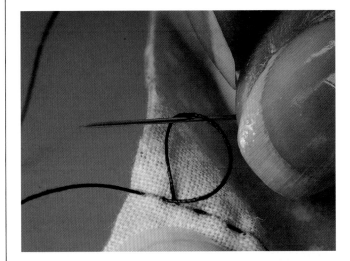

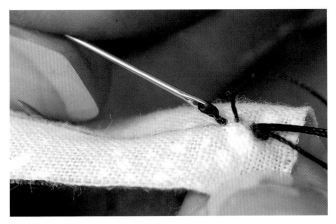

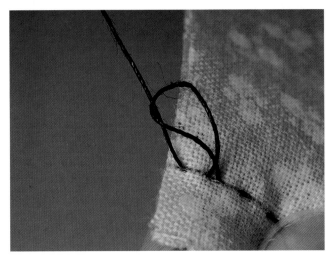

A backstitch loop in the seam every inch or so makes the seam stronger. This is especially important for larger projects, such as bed quilts, that get a lot of use.

Pull the needle and thread through the loop to make a knot.

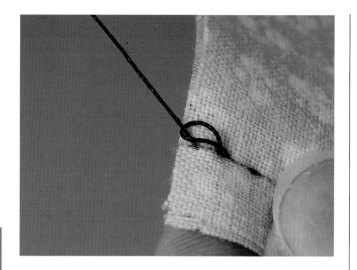

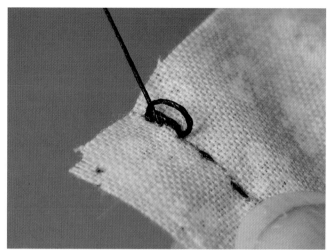

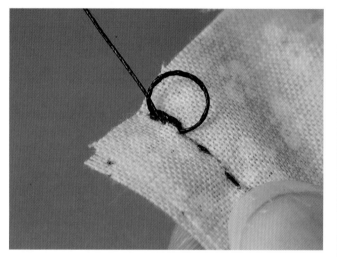

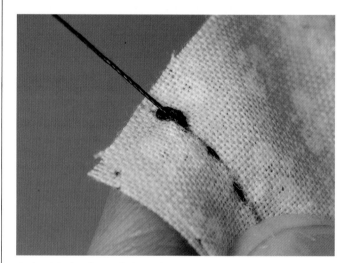

Make a second loop on top of the first one. Put the needle through this loop and pull the thread taut.

A double backstitch loop knot is very solid!

Running Stitch

This stitch can be used to sew pieces of fabric together and to quilt. Hold the needle the way that is comfortable for you. This usually is done with your thumb and several fingers holding the needle.

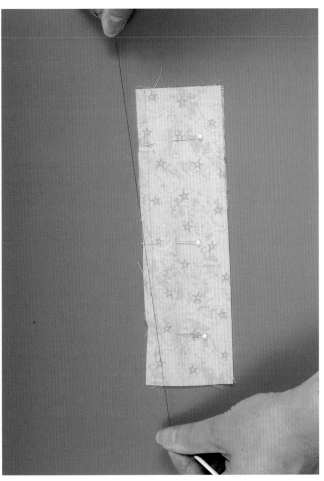

Cut a piece of thread three inches longer than the seam you're going to sew.

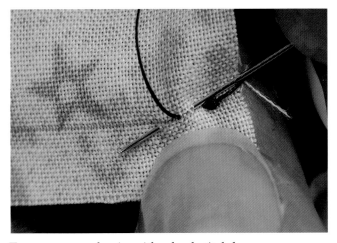

To sew a seam, begin with a backstitch loop.

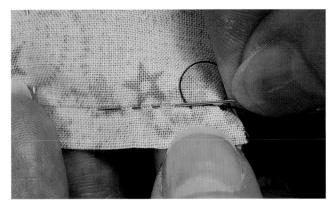

Then, hold the fabric smooth and flat with one hand and gently rock the tip of the needle up and down like a sailboat, catching a few threads of the top fabric and a few threads of the bottom fabric. Holding the fabric firmly makes this easier to do. You might also try pushing the fabric onto the needle with your other hand. Experiment and see how you prefer to do it.

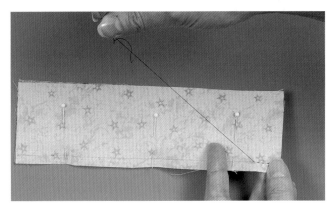

When you have three or four stitches on your needle, pull the thread all the way through.

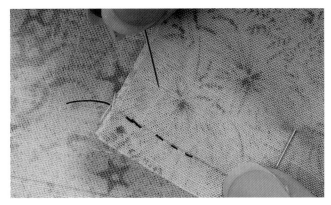

Smooth the fabric and look at your stitches. You want them to be about the same size on the top of the fabric and on the back side. It is okay if your stitches are large. It is more important to try to make them even (the same length) all along the seam.

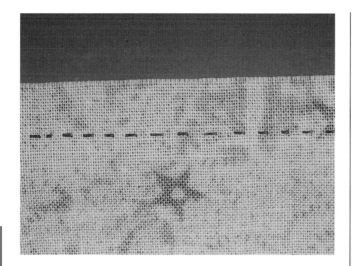

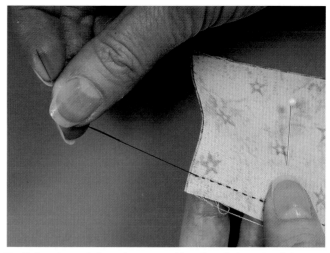

Pull the thread, but do not pull so hard that the fabric puckers. The fabric should lie flat and smooth.

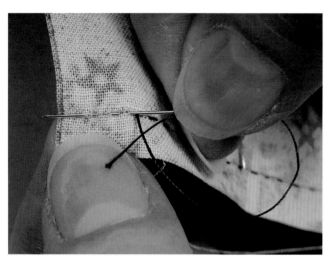

Before you get to the end of the seam, make sure you have enough thread to finish the seam and make the knot.

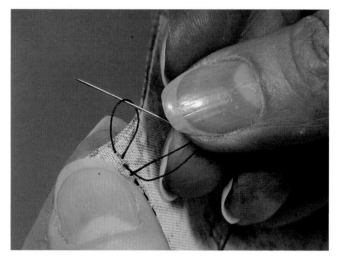

Continue in this way to the end of the seam and finish with a backstitch loop knot (see pages 19–20). Clip the thread $1/2$ to 1 inch away from the knot. As you can see, the back of your quilt will have lots of thread ends by the time you are finished sewing (piecing) it together. Keep the thread ends trimmed and neat. Another concern might be a long dark thread left on the quilt back that might show through a light fabric in the quilt block. It is very difficult to get inside a finished quilt to clip that thread. Best to do it now before the quilt is done.

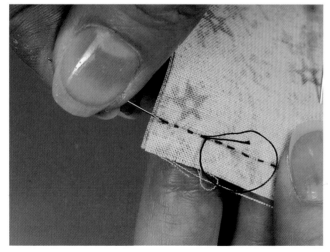

Finish the seam using the running stitch.

Rocking Stitch

This is another name for a running stitch that is used for quilting. It must be done differently because of the thickness of the quilt. You'll want a thimble to push the needle down through the three layers and back up again. Some people also wear a thimble on the other hand, which waits underneath the quilt to guide the needle back up to the surface.

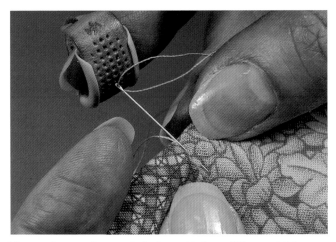

These photos show stitch-in-a-ditch quilting, which runs alongside the seams.

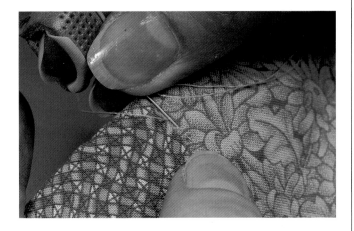

Holding the needle almost flat on the fabric, insert the tip until you feel it come through the back. The fingers

of the hand underneath guide the needle up through the fabric as the hand above presses down on the back of the needle to bring the tip up—rocking it up. Pick up three or four threads of the fabric in each stitch. Rock the needle back down into the fabric three or four threads away from where it came up.

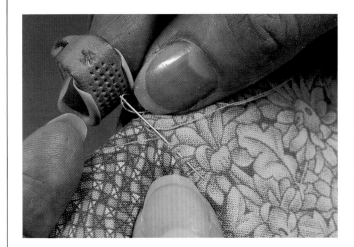

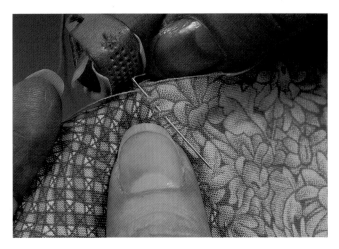

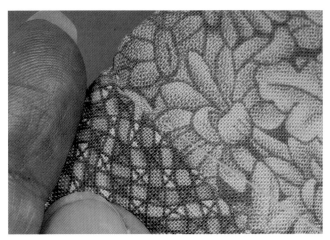

Run three or four stitches onto the needle before pulling the thread through.

You want to make stitches about the same size—the same size on the front and the back, too. This is challenging, so give yourself plenty of time to practice this stitch.

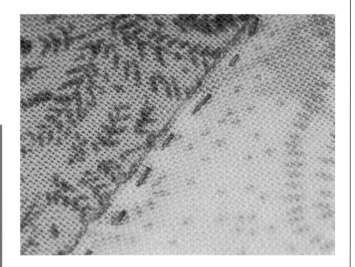

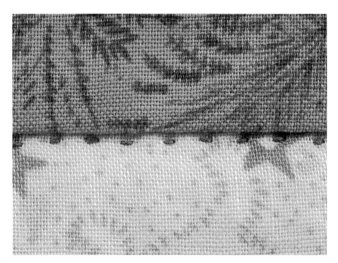

See how the stitches are even on the back and the front?

It is more important that stitches be the same size than it is to have small stitches. Don't be too concerned about it—enjoy your handiwork. Be sure to keep the fabric smooth on the top and bottom to help you stitch evenly. If the stitches are uneven or wander away from the stitching line, you can back up by removing the last stitches. Take the needle off the thread and pull the stitches out with the tip of the needle. Take your time and don't let the thread get tangled. When you have pulled out enough stitches to get back to the beginning or to where the stitches are even, you can smooth out the fabric, put the thread through the eye of the needle, and begin quilting again.

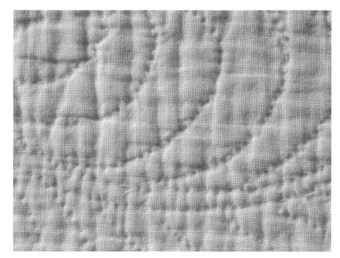

These stitches are on the back side of the quilt shown on page ii.

Stab Stitch

This stitch is good to use when you are stitching through seams or thick areas at the edge of a project.

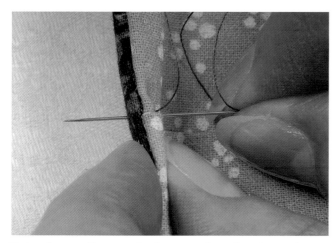

Point the needle straight down and push it through to the backside. The underneath hand pulls the needle and thread through the fabric.

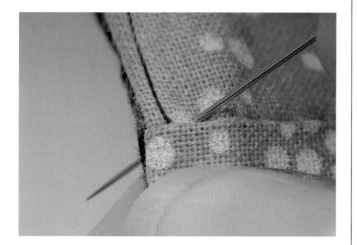

Turn the quilt over to see where the last stitch was made.

Pull the thread all the way through and then insert the needle close to where the thread came through from the other side. This will help you keep your stitches even.

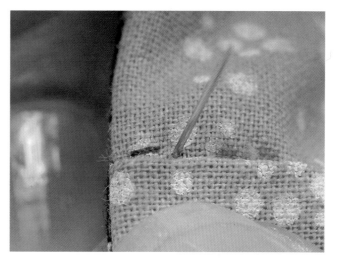

With each stitch, put the needle in the fabric close to the last stitch.

Blind Stitch

This stitch closes the edges of a project. It's called a blind stitch because you're not supposed to be able to see the stitches when you're done. Make the first stitch in the raw edge of the opening so the knot will not show when you've finished sewing the seam closed. See how the knot below is close to the raw edge of the fabric and well inside the seam line.

Hold the two edges together between your thumb and finger, and sew right along the seam line. You're just continuing the seam line. Take a stitch on one edge and then a stitch in the other, moving back and forth between the two.

When you pull the thread through, the seam closes and the stitches disappear inside.

Make a quilter's knot at the end of the seam and hide it inside, too (see pages 17–18).

Make three loops of thread around the needle.

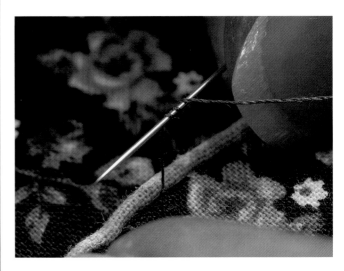

Keep the thread pulled snug as you insert the needle inside the seam.

Tug gently on the needle and thread until the knot slips inside the seam.

Bring the needle out farther along the seam line. Keep the loops tight on the needle as you pull the thread through.

Pull the thread tight and clip the thread very close to the seam. You should not see the knot or the end of the thread when you smooth out the fabric.

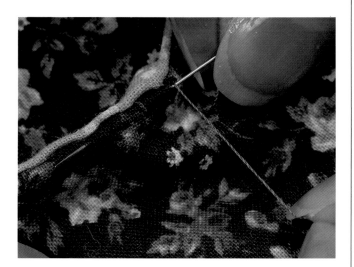

For large quilting projects, you will use a hoop or a frame to hold the part of the project that you are quilting. To quilt, you need the fabric to be smooth and flat and with a little tension on it. This makes it much easier to stitch through the layers with an even stitch. Hoops generally tighten on the fabric with a spring and screw. Square frames like this plastic one have removable sides that snap on over the fabric. Release the screw on the top hoop to loosen it so you can remove it from the bottom ring. Or pop off the pieces on each side of the frame.

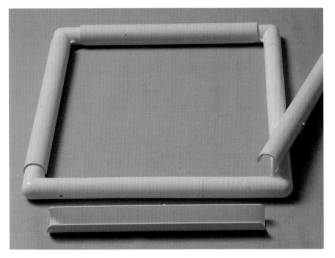

Place the quilt over the bottom ring. Smooth the layers. Check underneath to be sure the fabric is smooth there, too. Then snap the side pieces over the quilt or put the top ring over it and gently tighten the screw.

Check the underside again to be sure the fabric is smooth. Gently push up on the fabric in the frame to release some of the tension. You want it to move up an inch or two. If it's too tight, you won't be able to rock the needle.

Some quilt frames are as large as a king-sized quilt. The frame will fill up a room, but many people can work on the quilt at the same time. Or a few people can work without having to stop and move a smaller frame to another part of the quilt.

3

What Makes Up a Quilt

Most patchwork quilts are built on a block design. No matter which you choose, the pieces in each block are small enough to take with you and stitch anywhere. Stitching that you do during the minutes you might have to wait somewhere add up quickly. Of course, you can sew the pieces on a sewing machine if you have one, but try hand-sewing to see how you like it.

Most of the projects in this book are made from a single quilt block. To make larger quilts, you add blocks until the quilt is the size you want it to be. The table runner in this book has three blocks connected with sashing in between the blocks and a border running around the outside.

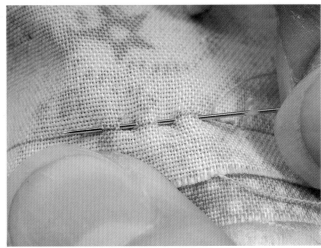

You can stitch any place, any time.

1. Choose the Quilt Block Pattern.

Many quilt blocks are built on squares, rectangles, and triangles. Curved edges are more difficult to sew because the edges stretch, so those shapes aren't included in this book.

SQUARES

The square is a basic form in a quilt block pattern. Four squares sewn together is called a Four Patch.

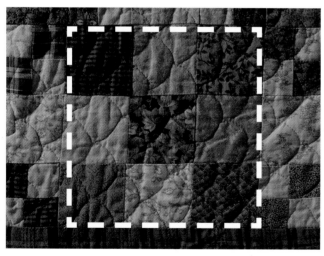

A Nine Patch is another basic block pattern. It has nine small squares sewn together in one block.

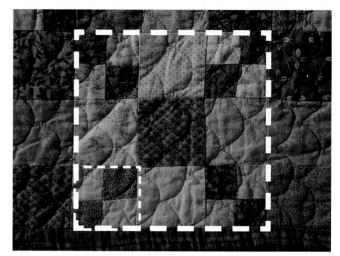

Some of the small squares in a Nine Patch can be divided again into a Four Patch.

RECTANGLES

You can sew rectangles together to make a block, as we do in the hot pad and three of the placemat designs.

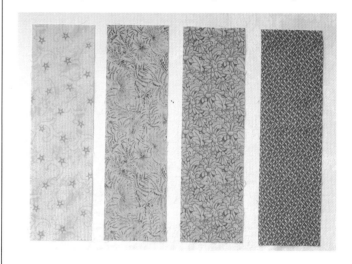

What Makes Up a Quilt

Safety

Quilting is not dangerous, but accidents can happen if you're careless with your scissors, rotary cutter, needles, or pins. When you are finished using it, make sure you put away everything that can cut you, and be aware of where it is until you put it away. Do not let anyone handle the rotary cutter, especially children.

If you are interrupted while you're stitching, slip the point of the needle into the fabric as though you were taking several running stitches. Leave the needle in the fabric to prevent it from getting lost or falling on the floor where someone might step on it. Fold the fabric over and around the needle, so it won't fall out.

A magnet is handy for finding a needle or pin that has gotten lost.

A Log Cabin block is a traditional pattern that uses squares and rectangles. It is said that during the Civil War, a black square in the middle indicated a safe house on the Underground Railroad, which was visible when the quilt was hanging on the clothesline. If the middle block was red, it was a warning not to approach the house at that time.

Amish quilts are well-known for the beauty of solid colors, simple shapes, and graceful quilting.

TRIANGLES

The easiest way to cut triangles is to cut a square into two triangles. This new shape provides variety in creating other quilt blocks.

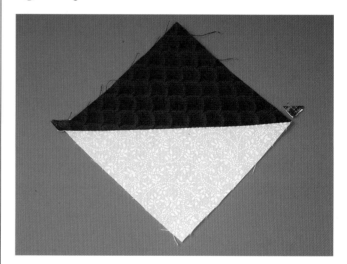

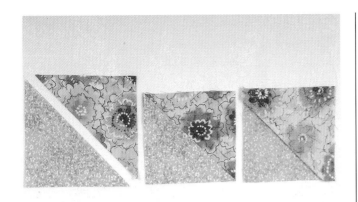

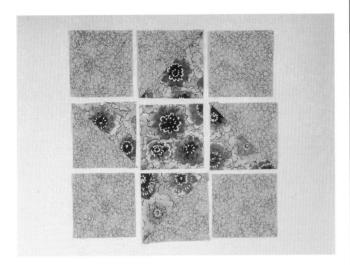

HEXAGONS—SIX-SIDED PIECES

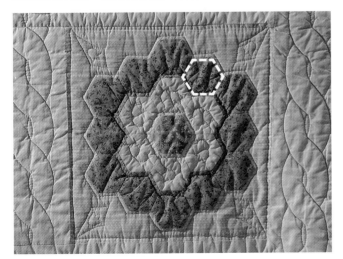

This quilt block is built with six-sided hexagons. The pattern is a traditional one called Grandmother's Flower Garden. To help keep the shape and make the corners crisp, quilters use paper or plastic templates that stay on the piece until they are all sewn together.

2. Piece the Quilt Top.

The next step is to cut out the pieces in the quilt block pattern. Then you sew the pieces together, being careful to check the block pattern after each seam. When you have finished piecing the top, you will cut the backing and then the batting. (We will discuss how to do this in the first project.) These are often referred to as the three parts of the "sandwich" of the finished quilt. The pieced block is on top, the batting in the middle, and the backing fabric is on the bottom.

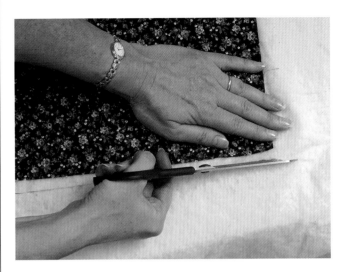

3. Quilt the Quilt.

Quilting is the stitching that adds texture and holds the three layers together. It dresses up plain sections of the quilt. As you quilt, hold the three pieces of the quilt together with large brass safety pins, making sure that the bottom layers are not creased or folded.

You also choose a pattern for the quilting: straight lines, which is the simplest quilting, or circles, flowers, hearts, or whatever you like. You may need a template to draw the quilting pattern on the fabric with a washable marker.

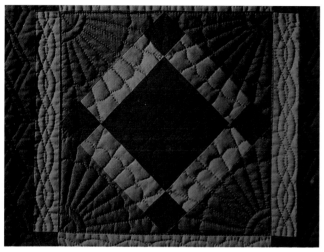

Note the quilting stitches on the blocks of solid color in this Amish quilt. The quilting is a very important part of the design.

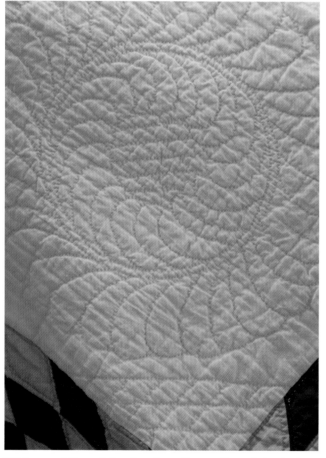

White on white quilting in a Lone Star quilt made in the late 1800s.

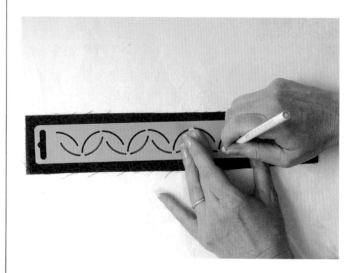

Preventing Fading from the Sun

After you spend time, money, and energy making a quilt, keep it out of the sun so the dark colors won't fade. Navy blues, in particular, fade easily. If they do fade, you will have gray pieces where the navy ones once were.

Note the navy blue swatch of material on the right side of the picture next to the Nine Patch block. The navy triangles on the top of the block are the same color as the original fabric. The gray triangles on the bottom corners used to be navy. The small squares in the middle of the block were navy once, too. Save yourself some heartache and frustration. Keep your quilt out of the sun—especially if it has navy blue in it.

FLOWERS

CHAIN STITCH QUILTING

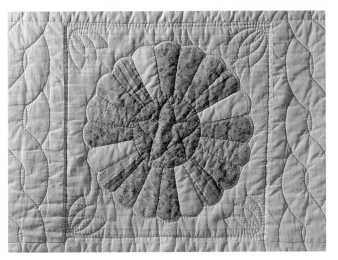

China Plate block with chain quilting

MORE FANCY QUILTING

STITCH IN THE DITCH

This stitch is the kindest quilting stitch for a beginner, because it's difficult for others to see. Stitching in the ditch means stitching right next to the seam line where the pieces of the block are sewn together.

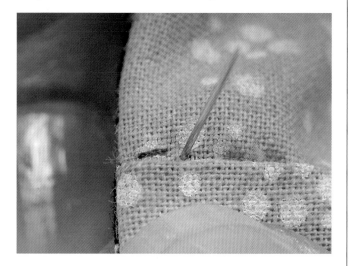

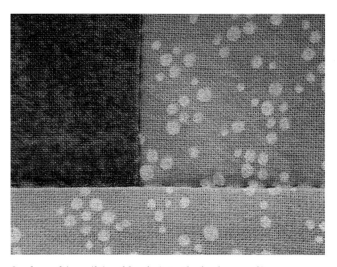

See how this quilting blends into the background?

OUTLINE QUILTING

Outline quilting is tracing the outline of the pieces in the design. It provides a nice finish and good foundation for other quilting in the block. You don't have to mark any lines for outline quilting.

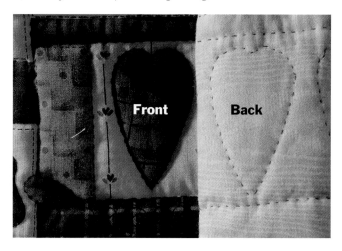

QUARTER-INCH QUILTING

This is stitching ¼ inch inside the seam line of each piece in the block. You probably won't need to mark the line for the quilting, but if you do, the seam provides a dependable guideline.

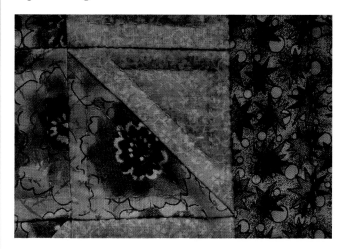

BACKGROUND QUILTING

Background quilting can be straight lines, double lines, or diamonds.

The simplest quilting pattern is an X on a square.

This is an example of diamond background quilting.

37

4

Understanding Fabric

Buy 100 percent cotton, the best fabric you can find to make your projects. You don't want permanent press or shiny treated cotton because it will be stiff and difficult to stitch. Thickness is the reason that corduroy, flannel, and felt are not good choices for you, not yet. Once you master the techniques, you will be able to include other fabrics, but nothing is better for the projects in this book than soft, well-woven cotton. The raw edges should not unravel easily, and you should not be able to see between the threads in the fabric.

Start with a Pattern

All quilters agree that choosing fabric is the greatest challenge. If you've never been in a fabric store before, you may be amazed at the number of fabrics, designs, and colors.

Don't panic. The simplest way is to start with one patterned or flowered fabric with colors you like. Then pick out two or three colors in the fabric that you want to match with other fabrics.

For example, the navy, blue, and pink flowered fabric is not the centerpiece, but it provides the reason for choosing pink and navy fabrics to go with it.

Lay the bolts of material on top of each other. Some solid colors will make the patterned fabric "pop," and others won't do anything for it. You won't know until you put them together. In this quilt to the right, the blue patterned fabric is matched with navy blue, light blue, and a crisp white.

Here the red Williamsburg print is matched with royal blue, light blue with yellow, and dark green fabric—all colors that are in the patterned fabric. The next two examples build on the patterned fabric.

Muted patterns can be treated like a solid color. The pink, blue, and orange batiks can go with the multicolored batik just as solid colors go with a flowered fabric.

This quilt is done in dusty shades of pink, green, and blue. There is no patterned fabric; the quilt is built on three shades of pink—light, medium, and dark. The pink is balanced by sage green and pale blue. The colors are serene, and the quilt blocks stand out.

42

Fat Quarters

You can buy fat quarters (or fat eighths) that have been packaged in colors that go together. Again, you see colors that are chosen to go with one or two patterned fabrics.

Four different fabrics from a package of fat quarters blend with a batik fabric containing those same colors.

Another approach is to choose dark, medium, and light colors. Light fabrics allow the block patterns to be seen clearly.

This is a Churn Dash block variation.

These colors were in one roll of fabrics cut in fat-quarter size.

These blocks alternate Duck's Foot with Bear Claw designs.

43

16 Triangles variation block.

Choose light, dark, medium—or match colors in the patterned fabric.

Have fun with your color choices—There is really no one right way to do it. This will bring out the artist in you!

These are all plaid fabrics, but they are pleasing together because of the muted forest colors and lots of beige.

Note that this queen-sized bed quilt is being quilted using a hoop. The safety pins and the hoop keep the three layers of the quilt from shifting around while you are stitching.

Fabric Know-How

SELVAGE
The finished edges of the fabric are the selvages. They may not have the same color as the rest of the fabric and are very tightly woven to prevent the fabric from unraveling.

You will cut the selvages off before you cut out any quilt pieces, because selvages are too stiff to stitch through.

You can cut the selvages off after you have cut out the piece—just be sure to move the template or the ruler over and begin measuring on the other side of the selvage.

Use the selvage as a guideline. It shows you the straight grain of the fabric. The straight grain runs parallel to the selvage or at a right angle across it. Cutting pieces on the grain keeps them from stretching out of shape and makes your quilt top sturdy.

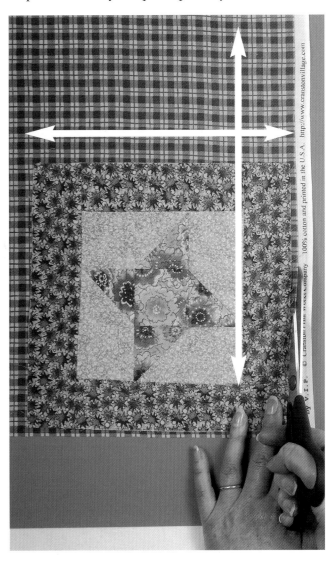

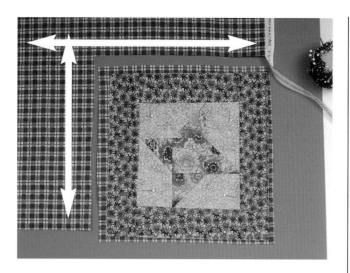

You want to cut along the straight grain of the fabric so the pieces will be sturdy and keep their shape.

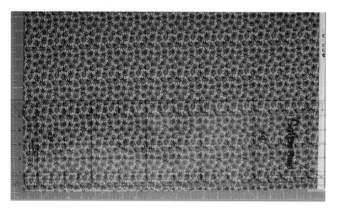

Fabric stretches if you cut diagonally across the grain. This is called the "bias" of the fabric. If you cut pieces on the bias, they will stretch out of shape, but if you try to stretch fabric on the straight grain, it will not move at all.

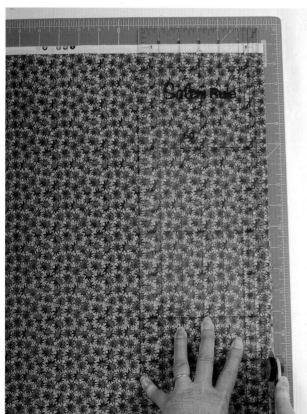

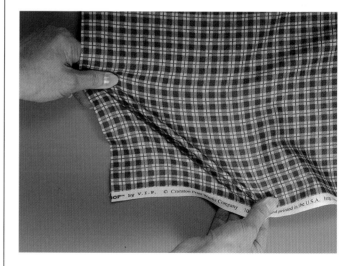

Clean up any uneven edges before you start cutting pieces for the block.

RAW EDGES

The cut edge of the fabric is called the raw edge. When you sew a seam, line up the edges and pin them together. Then sew along the marked seam line.

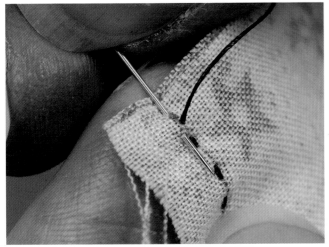

If the fabric frays badly and all those threads get in your way, you may want to try another fabric—one that does not unravel so easily. As you can see in the photo, a little fraying is to be expected. Be careful not to pull on the raw edges, which makes fraying worse.

RIGHT AND WRONG SIDE

Notice the right and the wrong side of the fabric. The colors on the right side are usually brighter, and the pattern is clearer. The wrong side is pale in comparison to the right side and sometimes has different threads or patterns.

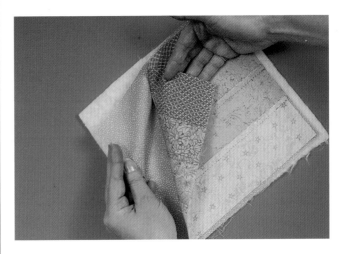

BACKING FABRIC

If you don't want your quilting stitches to show on the back, choose a patterned or floral fabric for the backing. Use thread that blends in with the fabric.

Historically, people used plain muslin for a backing, but it's not very exciting. Try one of the fabrics in the quilt top or another coordinating color for the backing. By doing this, you may enjoy the back of your quilt almost as much as the front.

47

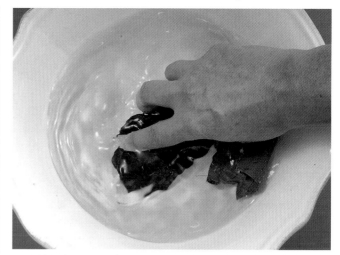

Cut the backing fabric larger than the quilt top. If you are making a large quilt, allow two or more inches extra fabric all around.

Check to see if the dye in the fabric will run.

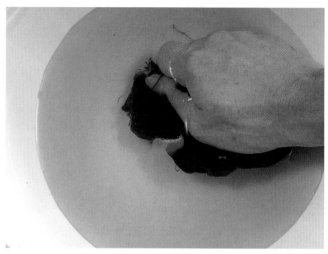

PRE-WASH YOUR FABRIC BEFORE CUTTING

Unfold the fabric, and use cold water and a mild detergent or sudsy ammonia. If you wash it folded, the fabric on the fold may fade. The point of washing the fabric before you cut it is to remove some of the dye and to keep the dark colors from bleeding onto the light colors in the finished quilt. You can wash the fabrics by hand or in the washing machine on a gentle cycle. If you have a dark colored fabric, dip it into cold water and see whether it leaves dye in the water. If it colors the water, don't wash it with the other fabrics or the dye may run and stain them. If you put the fabric in two or three changes of clean water and the dye keeps running, don't use that fabric in your quilt.

Note that the dye colors the water. If you dunk this fabric in clean water again, the excess dye should be gone and the water should stay clear.

Dry the fabric on a permanent press setting. Iron out any wrinkles.

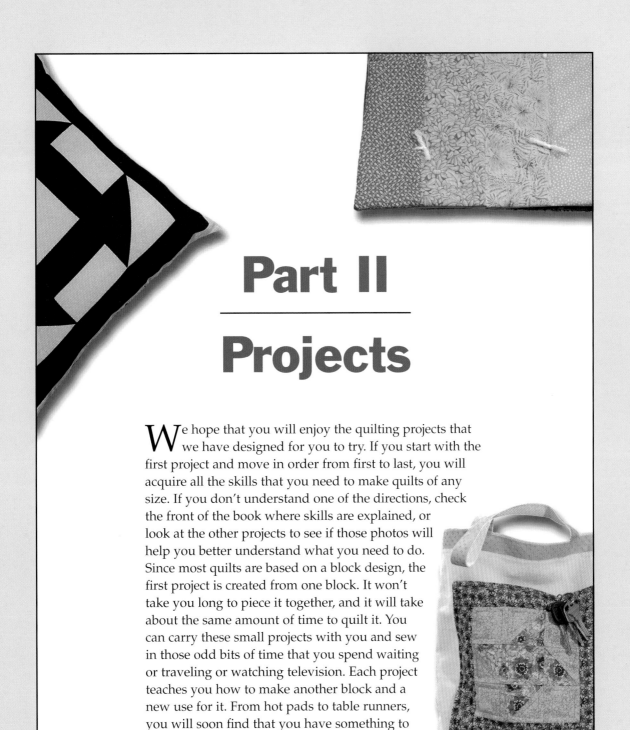

Part II

Projects

We hope that you will enjoy the quilting projects that we have designed for you to try. If you start with the first project and move in order from first to last, you will acquire all the skills that you need to make quilts of any size. If you don't understand one of the directions, check the front of the book where skills are explained, or look at the other projects to see if those photos will help you better understand what you need to do. Since most quilts are based on a block design, the first project is created from one block. It won't take you long to piece it together, and it will take about the same amount of time to quilt it. You can carry these small projects with you and sew in those odd bits of time that you spend waiting or traveling or watching television. Each project teaches you how to make another block and a new use for it. From hot pads to table runners, you will soon find that you have something to show for your time and creative energies. Caution: Quilting has been shown to be addictive!

5

Hot Mat or Pot Holder

New Skills

- How to cut a template
- How to cut fabric pieces
- How to sew seams with a running stitch
- How to press seams
- How to layer backing, batting, and quilt top
- How to finish the edges
- How to bury the knot in the batting
- How to quilt with "stitch in the ditch"
- How to tie a quilt

SHOPPING LIST
Hot Mat or Pot Holder

Item & Quantity

- [ ] Fabric, 5 fat eighths or $1/8$ yard of 5 colors

- [ ] Batting, 12-inch square for each hot mat
  Heat-resistant batting, thin- or medium-weight cotton

- [ ] Thread, sewing and quilting
  Color to match the fabric

- [ ] Needles, betweens and sharps 10, 11, or 12

- [ ] Brass safety pins, 1 package

- [ ] Pins, 1 package

- [ ] Template plastic, 1 $8^1/2$ x 11-inch sheet

- [ ] Scissors

- [ ] Clear ruler

- [ ] Mechanical pencil

- [ ] Thimble

- [ ] Iron

- [ ] Pinking shears, optional

HOT MAT / POT HOLDER TEMPLATE
$2^1/2$ x $8^1/2$-inch Rectangle

Block Name: Four-Bar Block

Makes four hot mats or pot holders or two "tied" pot holders

If you don't use heat-resistant batting and want to get maximum protection from your pot holder, you can tie two finished hot mats together—another classic quilting technique used with comforters. Then you can safely lift hot pans and protect yourself from getting burned.

Hot Mat or Pot Holder

1. Choose your fabric. Rolls of fat eighths have five co-ordinating colors packaged for you. You just have to pick colors you like!

2. Unfold and wash the fabrics in cold water. Dry on permanent press, and iron out any wrinkles in the fabric.

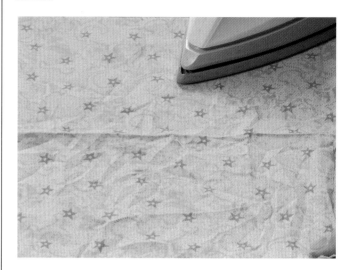

3. You'll need to make a template for cutting out the pieces of fabric for the quilt block. You will need four rectangles of different colors for this project. The backing fabric can be cut after you finish piecing together the top. The quilt top becomes the template for cutting the backing to fit it.

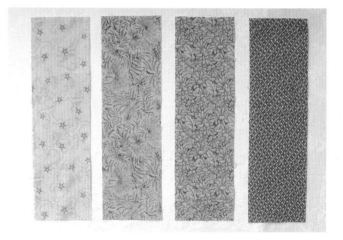

4. You can make a template one of two ways. Trace the rectangular pattern on page 51 onto a sheet of template plastic with a permanent marker.

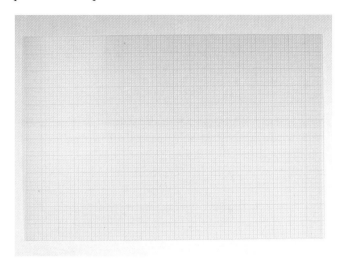

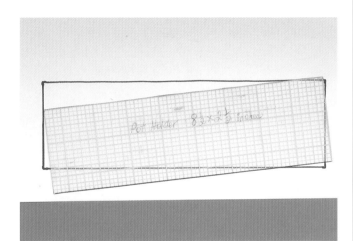

Or use a ruler to measure the rectangle on the template plastic. The rectangle is $8^{1}/_{2}$ inches long and $2^{1}/_{2}$ inches wide. Mark the lines on the plastic.

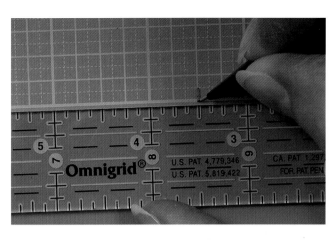

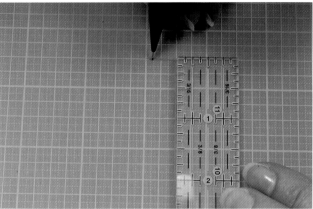

Cut out the template.

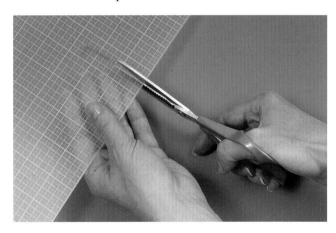

Label it with the name of the quilt block.

5. You can place the template over the one in the book to be sure you have cut it out accurately.

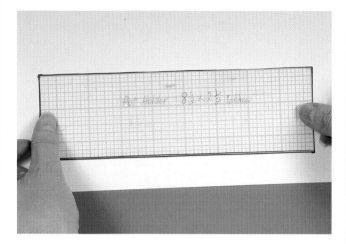

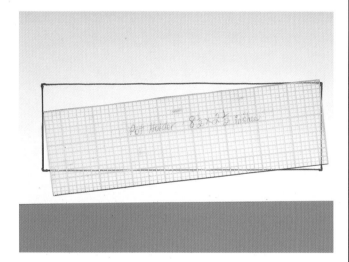

6. Separate the fabrics to be sure you know which pieces to cut out of each color. Lay the fabric on a flat work surface. Be careful not to scratch the table or floor beneath the fabric with the scissors. You could protect it with cardboard or thick paper.

You need four rectangles, one of each color. The fabric in fat quarters should have been cut on the straight grain of the fabric. All you need to do is put the long edge of your template along the longer edge of the fabric. If you use other fabric, the selvage is the stiff woven edge. Move your template to avoid any of the selvage. See page 45 for more information about the grain of the fabric. Trace the template onto the fabric using a mechanical pencil or other marker.

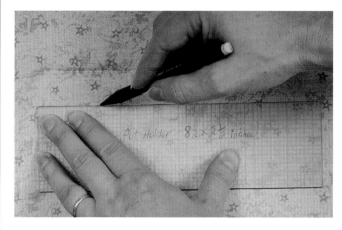

You should be able to see the outline of the template.

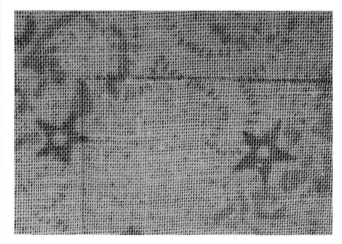

Cut out the fabric pieces for your project.

7. If you have a rotary cutter, use the special cutting board to protect the work surface. A rotary cutter is extremely sharp and can cut through cardboard and carpet. If you try to cut on plywood or tile, you may dull the blade of the cutter.

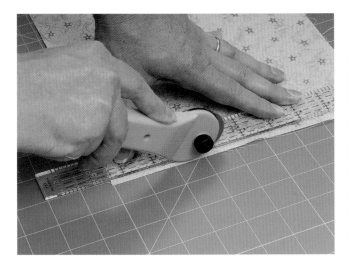

Press down firmly on the ruler or template and the fabric to keep them from sliding around.

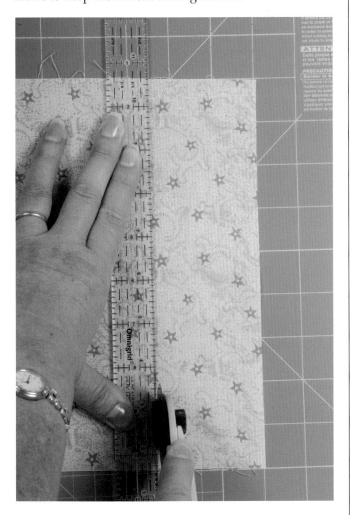

Always cap the blade as soon as you are finished cutting.

8. Lay out the pieces in the block pattern. Seeing it helps you keep track of where you are and which pieces need to be sewn to each other.

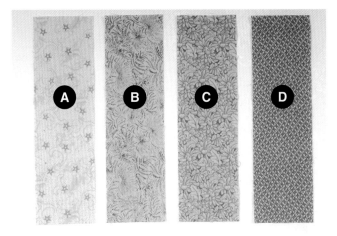

9. Mark the seam line ¼ inch from the edges of the fabric, using a clear ruler and a mechanical pencil or other easily erased marker. It is important to sew on these straight lines, so the block pattern fits together correctly.

Mark seam lines on all edges.

10. Pin the first two pieces of fabric together with right sides together and the raw edges aligned.

Check again to be sure the right sides of both peices are facing each other. The right side usually has brighter colors.

Place pins about 3 inches apart.

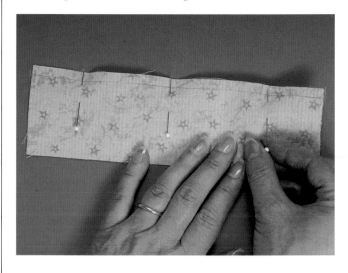

The points of the pins run along the seam you will be sewing.

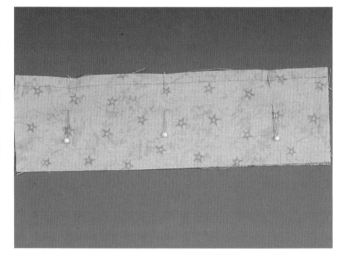

You are going to sew piece A to B, and then sew C to D.

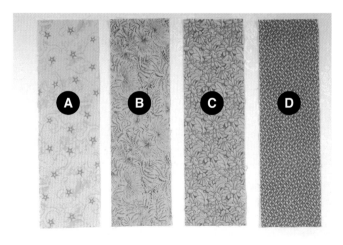

11. Cut a piece of thread about three inches longer than the seam you are going to sew. Thread the needle.

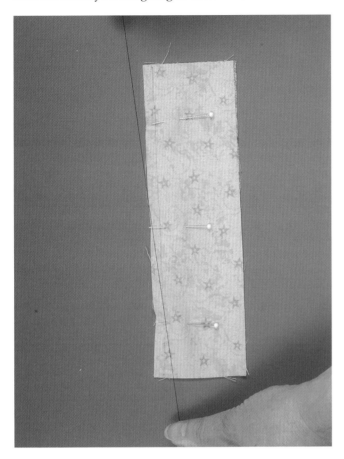

Tie a knot in the thread. (See pages 14–15.) Hold the end of the thread against the needle, and with the other hand, wrap the thread three times around the needle. Pinch the three loops between your thumb and finger as the other hand pulls the needle through the loops. Keep holding the loops and slide them all the way to the end of the thread.

12. Make the first stitch close to the edge of the fabric.

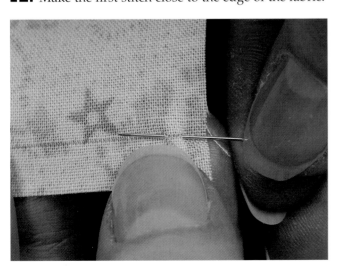

Pull the thread through the fabric slowly until the knot touches the fabric. Do not pull it too tight or the seam will pucker and not lay flat.

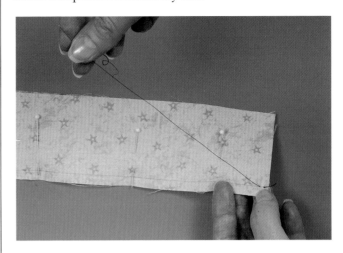

13. Make a backstitch over the first stitch.

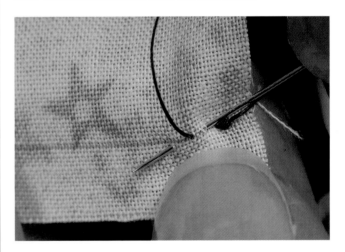

Run three to five stitches onto the needle and pull the thread through the fabric. Continue sewing the seam with the running stitch (see pages 21–22).

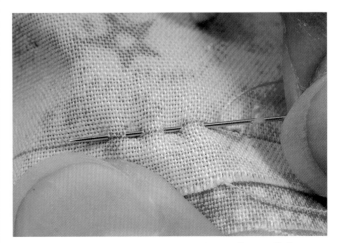

Big stitches are okay, just try to keep them all the same size.

57

14. Check often to be sure that you are stitching along the sewing line on both the bottom and the top pieces.

15. When you come to the end of the seam, make a backstitch loop by taking the needle back through the last stitch, leaving a loop of thread. (See page 19.)

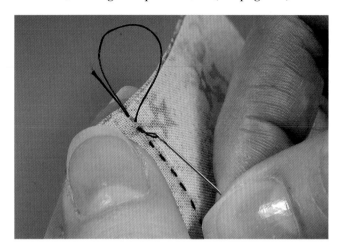

Put the needle through the loop and pull the thread tight to make a knot. Clip off the extra thread.

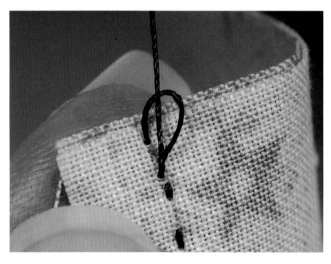

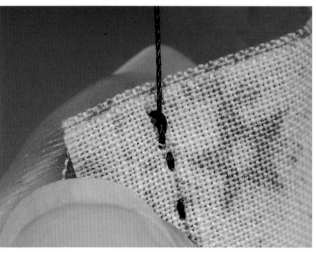

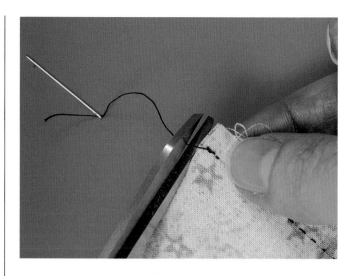

Iron the seams toward the darker fabric (see page 10.)

16. Put the sewn pieces (A + B and C + D) back into the block to be sure they have gone together the way you expected them to.

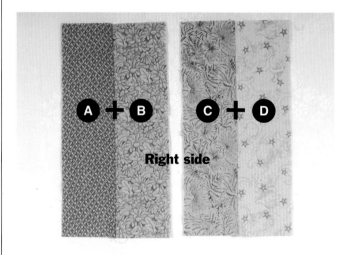

The raw edges of the seams can be seen on the wrong side of the pieced block. Note that the seams are pressed toward the darker fabric.

17. Now sew the two larger sections (A + B and C + D) together.

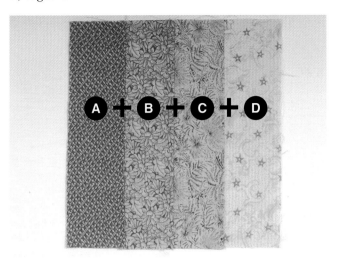

Iron all the raw edges of the seams toward the darker fabrics.

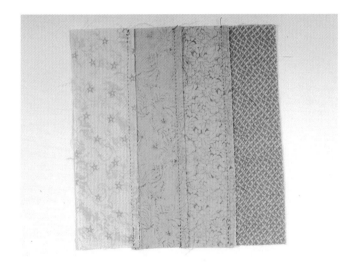

A mistake that *all* quilters make is sewing the right side of one piece to the wrong side of another. Take the time to double-check before you sew them together. It saves time and having to rip it out later.

18. Mark a $^{1}/_{4}$-inch seam allowance around the pieced top using a clear ruler and a pencil.

Mark the line on the wrong side of the fabric.

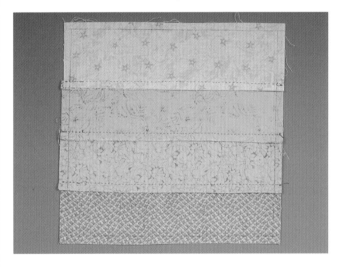

When you get ready to assemble the quilt, you'll be able to see the stitching line.

19. Now cut the backing fabric, using the quilt top as a template. Lay the quilt top on the backing fabric along the selvage or straight grain. Pin them together and cut, leaving about $\frac{1}{2}$ inch extra backing fabric all around the outside of the quilt top.

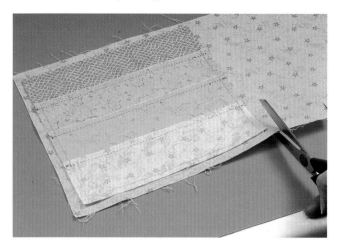

Next, use the backing as a template to cut the batting. Pin the backing to the batting to keep it from sliding, if you wish. There is no grain to the batting.

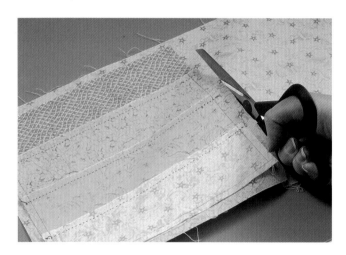

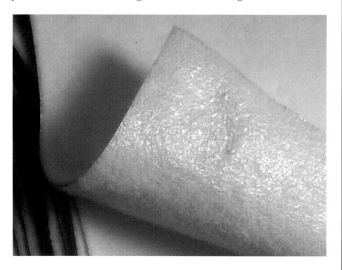

When you are finished cutting, you will have a backing and a batting piece to go inside the quilt.

20. There are three layers in a quilt: backing, batting, and top. But for this project, we must stack them on the work surface in this order: (1) the batting, (2) the backing, with the right side facing up toward you, and (3) the quilt block with the wrong side facing you. You see the raw seam edges. The right sides of the backing and the quilt top face each other on the inside.

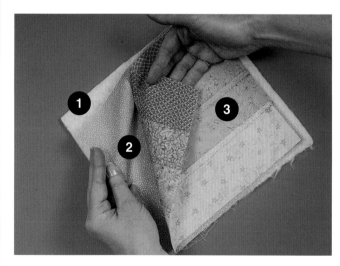

Again, take the time to double-check the order of the three parts and that the right sides of the fabric are together.

21. Pin the three layers together with brass safety pins. Place a pin every 3 or 4 inches all over the quilt. The more pins you use, the less chance the layers will move around while you are stitching.

22. You will sew around the outer edge of the hot pad, but leave a 3-inch opening in the seam. This will allow you to turn the hot mat right-side out. Mark the opening with pins, so you don't forget and sew it closed.

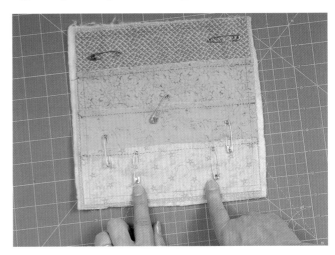

23. Following the ¼-inch seam line, sew the three layers together with regular thread using a running stitch. Start at the pin marking the opening with a backstitch loop to anchor your stitching.

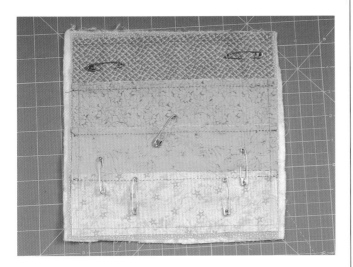

61

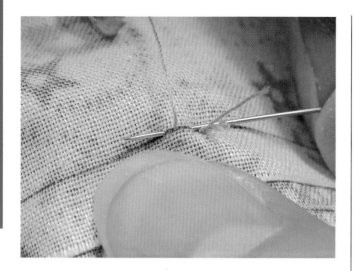

Stitch along the seam line you marked earlier. Use a running stitch (page 21) or whatever works for you.

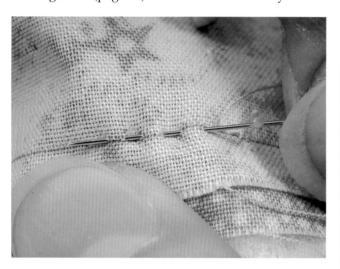

At the corner, be sure the stitch ends exactly at the corner, and then turn the quilt so you can sew down the next side. You could do a backstitch at the corners to make them stronger.

24. When you reach the pin at the other side of the 3-inch opening, end the seam with a double backstitch loop knot (see pages 19–20).

25. Trim the edges of the hot mat with pinking shears, if you have them. This helps prevent the fabric from unraveling. If you do not have pinking shears, trim the batting and backing with scissors so they are nearly the same size as the quilt top. This removes excess bulk, so the hot mat will lay flat, and you won't have to quilt through six layers around the outside edges.

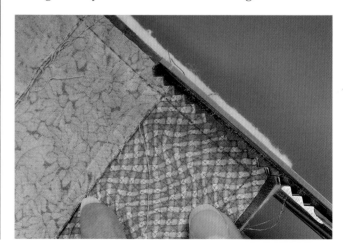

Remove the safety pins from the trimmed block with the 3-inch opening.

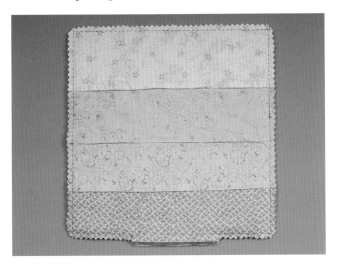

26. Push the inside of the hot mat up through the opening to turn it inside out. Now the right side of the pieced top and the backing is outside, and the batting is sandwiched inside.

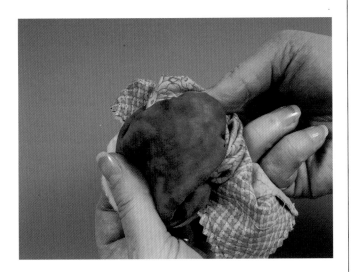

Push all layers gently through the opening.

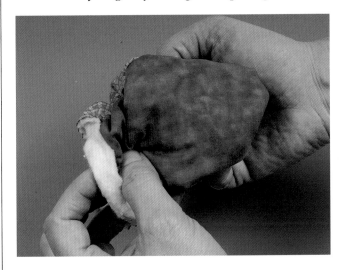

27. The corners of the hot mat may not be square, so push them out gently with a pencil, knitting needle, or crochet hook. Be careful not to push through the fabric.

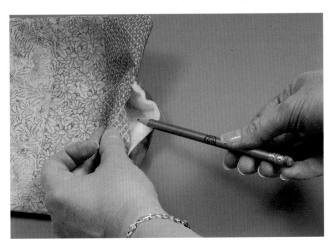

Try to make to corners square.

28. Trim any batting that may be sticking out of the opening.

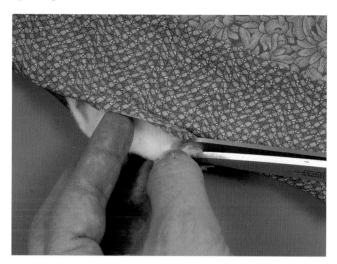

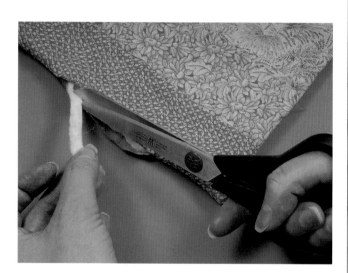

Finger-press the raw edges of the seam inside the opening.

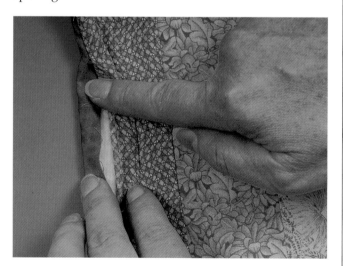

Iron the hot mat, taking care to press under the seam allowance at the opening.

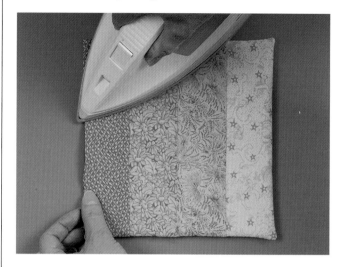

29. Pin the opening closed. Sew it closed with a blind stitch (see pages 26–27). Start with a needle and about 10 inches of thread. Make a knot at one end of the thread. Pull the needle through the raw edges so the knot will be hidden inside the seam. To blind stitch, hold the two edges of the seam together between thumb and forefinger and go from side to side with the needle, taking a stitch in each. Pull gently to close the opening. To finish make a quilter's knot and bury it in the batting so all you see is the finished seam.

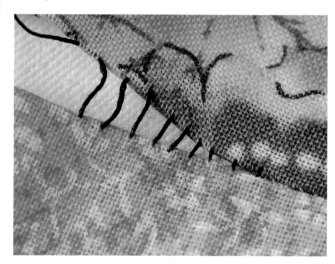

You can press the block now and put safety pins in it to hold the three layers together while you quilt.

30. Now it's time to quilt the hot mat by stitching through all three layers. In this project, you "stitch in the ditch," meaning you will stitch right next to the seams in the quilt block. This is the most common way of quilting, and it is kind to beginners because it is difficult for others to see the stitches. You'll need thimbles or leather pads, because the needle is guided by your fingertips.

Stitch along one side of each seam in the block.

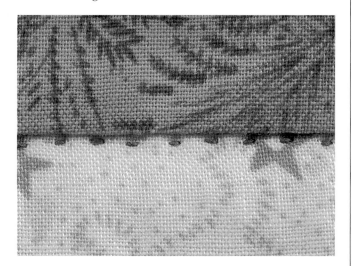

31. Choose a neutral color or a color that matches your fabric for your quilting thread. Cut a 20-inch piece of quilting thread and thread the "between" needle. Make a quilter's knot at the end of the thread (see pages 14–15).

32. Bury the knot in the batting layer. Put the needle in the quilt top approximately $1/2$ inch away from where you are going to start quilting. (Don't go through the backing fabric.) The tip of the needle comes up right at the seam. Pull the thread until the knot touches the quilt top. Pull gently on the thread until the knot slips through the fabric. Stop pulling! You want the knot to stay inside in the batting layer (see page 16).

33. The needle is on top of the quilt block. Insert the needle close to the seam and push it straight down to the backside. Pull it through with your other hand, and turn the fabric over to see that the fabric is smooth. Put the needle in close to the first stitch and push it straight up through the fabric. This is called the stab stitch. This stitch is good to use when you have thick areas to go through like those at the edge of the hot mat. (See page 25.)

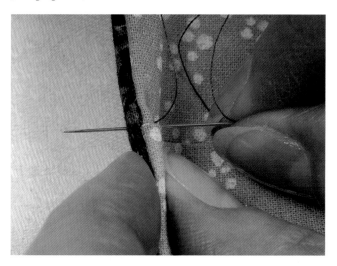

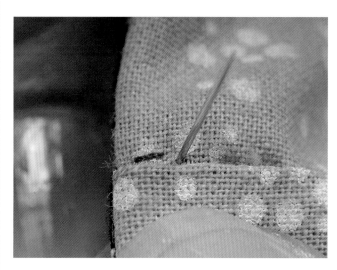

Away from the thick edges, you can use a running or rocking stitch, called that because you "rock" the needle like a sailboat up and down, catching a few threads above and a few below until you have three or four stitches on the needle (see pages 23–24).

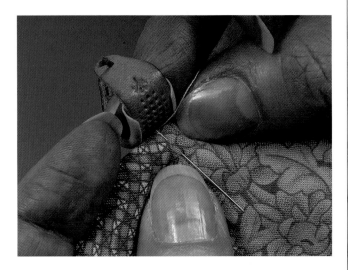

Make sure that fabric underneath is smooth and not bunched up.

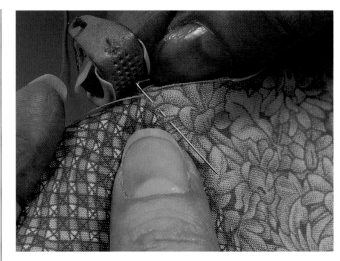

You can see how a thimble helps protect your finger as you push the needle through all the layers.

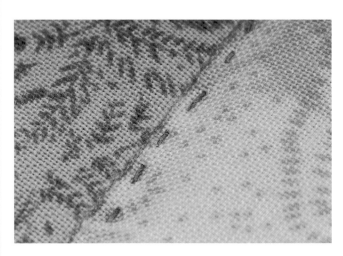

34. At the end of the seam, finish by making a quilter's knot and burying it in the batting layer (see pages 17–18).

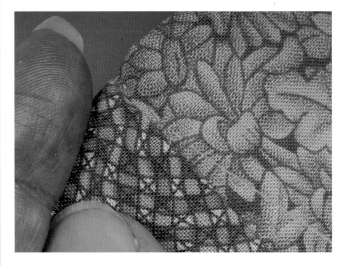

Quilt along each of the seams in the block using the same techniques.

New Skill: How to Tie a Quilt

If you don't use heat-resistant batting in your hot mat, you can still set hot things on it, but it will be too thin to protect your hand when removing a hot pan from the oven. For a thicker pot holder, you can tie two finished hot mats together. Larger tied quilts are called comforters and usually have thick batting—too thick to quilt through. The ties hold the batting in place.

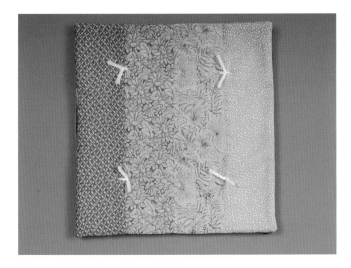

To make a tied hot mat, you'll need a 30-inch length of yarn. Needle-nose pliers will help you pull the yarn through the quilt more easily.

1. Thread a large needle with yarn. (Hint: Fold a piece of thread in half and put the loop into the eye of needle. Put the end of the yarn through the loop. Pull the thread and the yarn back through the eye of the needle. You can also try using a needle threader like the wire one on page 3.)

2. Mark where you want the ties to be—at least four in a block the size of the hot mat. Leave a 3- to 4-inch tail of yarn at each stitch so you can tie it in a knot.

Note the 3-inch piece of yarn.

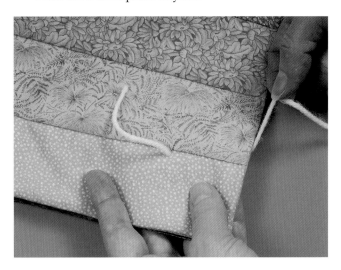

You can use a pair of needle-nose pliers to pull the yarn through the thickness of two mats.

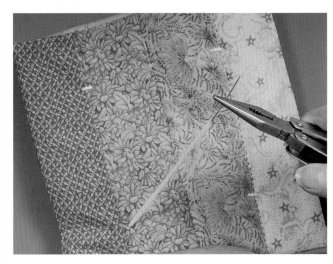

3. Make the three other stitches where the ties will be before you cut the yarn.

Do not pull the yarn tight between the stitches. You need to leave extra yarn so you'll have enough to tie the knots.

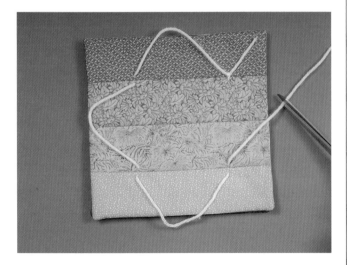

Clip the yarn, leaving a 3-inch tail at the end. Then clip the yarn between the stitches.

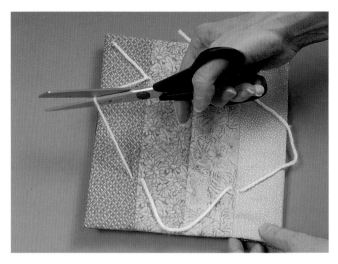

4. Tie the ends of the yarn for each tie in a square knot. To tie a square knot, take the yarn in your right hand over the yarn in your left hand.

Pull that knot closed. Then take the yarn in your left hand over the yarn in your right hand.

Pull the knot closed.

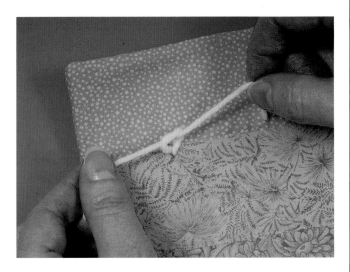

Then cut the excess yarn about 1 inch from each knot. You can expect some unraveling of the yarn.

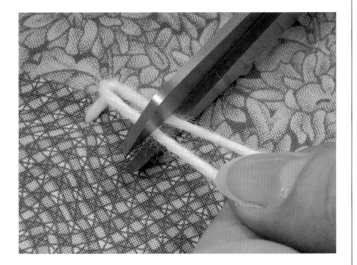

This is how the ties look on the back side.

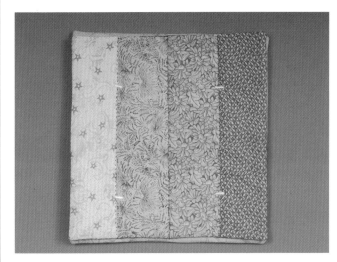

Your hot mat or pot holder is now thick enough to protect your hands and your tabletop from hot dishes.

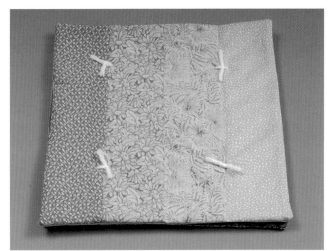

69

6

Placemats

New Skills

- Four new quilt block patterns
- How to join pieces that have seams

The directions for each block pattern make four place-mats—one for each season of the year.

Rail Fence: Summer

(three colors: purple, lavender, blue)

FABRIC

Light:	16 x 45 inches
Medium:	16 x 45 inches
Dark:	16 x 45 inches
Backing:	28 x 45 inches

Five-Bar: Fall
(four colors: green, two oranges, yellow)

FABRIC

Yellow:	20 x 45 inches
Green:	20 x 45 inches
Orange:	20 x 45 inches
Center print:	10 x 45 inches
Backing:	28 x 45 inches

(The backing can be one of the fabrics used on the top.)

71

SHOPPING LIST
Placemats

Item & Quantity

☐ Fabric, varies by block pattern

☐ Batting, thin- or medium-weight, 28 x 45 inches

☐ Thread, sewing and quilting Color to match the fabric

☐ Needles, betweens and sharps 10, 11, or 12

☐ Brass safety pins, 1 package

☐ Pins, 1 package

☐ Template plastic, 2 sheets (8½ x 11-inches)

☐ Scissors

☐ Clear ruler

☐ Mechanical pencil

☐ Thimble

☐ Iron

Nine-Patch: Winter (Christmas)
(three colors: white, red, green)

FABRIC
Light:	20 x 45 inches
Dark:	20 x 45 inches
Backing:	28 x 45 inches

Streaks of Lightning: Spring
(two colors: green, yellow flowers)

FABRIC
Print fabric:	20 x 45 inches
Solid fabric:	20 x 45 inches
Backing:	28 x 45 inches

72

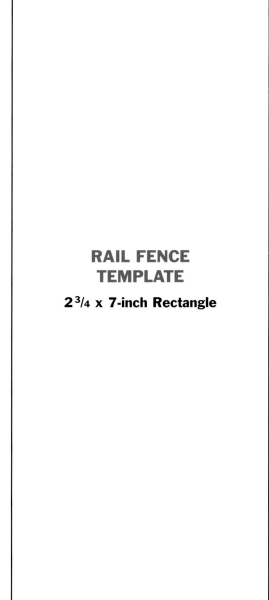

**RAIL FENCE
TEMPLATE**

2 $^{3}/_{4}$ x 7-inch Rectangle

**FIVE-BAR
TEMPLATE**

2 $^{1}/_{4}$ x 20-inch Rectangle

Enlarge 200%

**NINE-PATCH
TEMPLATE**

4 $\frac{1}{2}$-inch Square

**STREAKS OF
LIGHTNING
TEMPLATE**

2 $\frac{1}{2}$ x 4 $\frac{1}{2}$-inch Rectangle

1. Choose your fabric. You'll need three colors for the Rail Fence placemats. We chose dark blue with purple flowers and two different purple fabrics to match.

2. Unfold and wash the fabrics in cold water—one at a time, in case one bleeds its color. Check for dye in the water. Dry on the permanent press setting and iron out wrinkles before cutting.

3. Use the selvages to find the straight grain of the fabric and the direction in which you will trace and cut your pieces. See page 45 for more about the straight grain of the fabric.

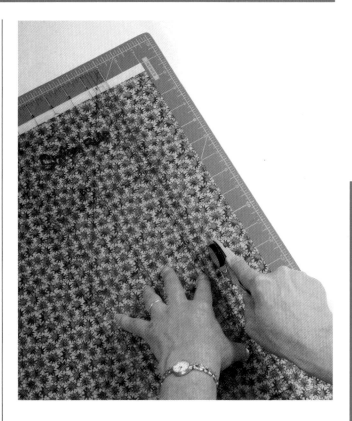

4. Trace the rectangle on page 73 to make a plastic template for the block pattern, or use a ruler and these dimensions ($2^3/_4$ x 7 inches) to draw your own. You will be cutting all the pieces for the Rail Fence placemat—six rectangles of each of the three colors—using this template. Place the template on the fabric along the straight grain. Trace around it.

5. Cut out the pieces for the front of the placemat. Mark a stitching line $1/_4$ inch from the edges of all the pieces, using a clear ruler and a mechanical pencil or other marker (see page 55).

6. Each small block in the pattern is the same. Pin the first two pieces of fabric with right sides together (A to B, then A + B to C) and the raw edges aligned. Sew with regular thread using a running stitch. Start and end with a backstitch knot (see pages 19–20). Sew one dark, one medium, and one light rectangle side by side.

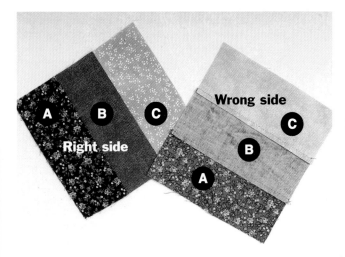

7. When all six blocks are completed, use an iron to press the seams toward the darker color.

The six small blocks are all the same.

8. The design depends on how you lay the blocks out. Each block is placed in the pattern in a different direction.

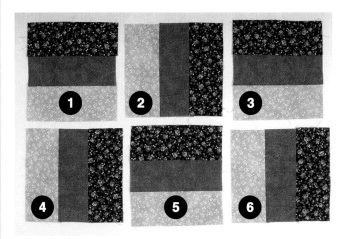

9. Now it's time to sew the six small blocks together to get three larger blocks that become 1 of the 3 rows in the pattern. Sew two small blocks together to make a row. Lay them back in the pattern to make sure that you are sewing the correct pieces together. When you've finished sewing these three larger blocks, press the new seams with an iron.

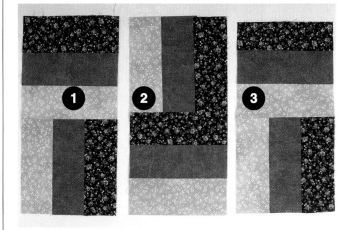

76

10. Pin two of the rows with right sides together, making sure the seams meet perfectly.

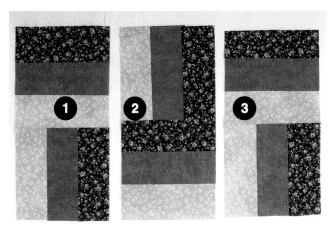

You want the dark piece on the bottom to meet the dark piece in the middle. Use lots of pins to hold the seams in place. This is important for the final look of your placemats. With all the seams matching, you will feel so much better about your work. Pin the third row to the large block, and sew. This completes the top of your placemat.

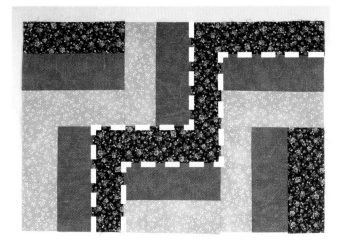

Here's how the wrong side will look.

11. Press all the seams toward the dark fabric.

12. Mark a $1/4$-inch seam line all around the outside of the top. Use a clear ruler and a mechanical pencil or another easily erased marker. This line will help you sew straight and even seams.

13. Lay the pieced top on the backing fabric and cut around it, leaving an extra inch of the backing fabric. Then use the backing fabric as a template to cut the batting.

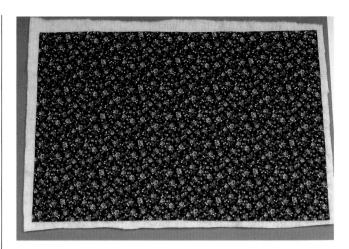

Make the batting at least $1/2$ inch larger than the backing piece.

14. Now stack the three pieces of the quilt. First, the batting. Second, the backing fabric with the right side facing up. Third, the pieced top with the wrong side facing you. The right sides of the backing and the quilt top face each other.

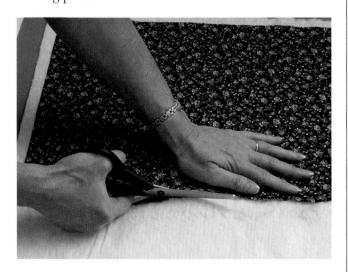

15. Pin the three layers together carefully.

As you are pinning, be sure that the three layers are not bunched up. Smooth them flat and then pin through all three layers.

Leave a 3-inch opening in the middle of the seam on one of the long sides. Mark this opening with pins so you don't forget to keep it open.

If you had trouble getting the hot mat through a 3-inch opening, you may want to make this one 4 or 5 inches long. Keep away from the corners.

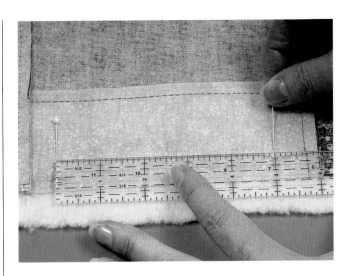

16. Sew around the outside edge of the placemat using a running stitch and make backstitch loops along the seam to strengthen it. Leave the opening so you can turn the placement right-side out.

17. Use pinking shears or scissors to trim the edges of the placemat.

Trim at the opening, too. Remove all the pins.

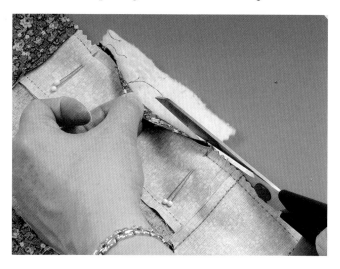

18. Turn the placemat inside out by pushing it up through the opening. The right side of the quilt top and the backing are showing, and the batting is sandwiched inside.

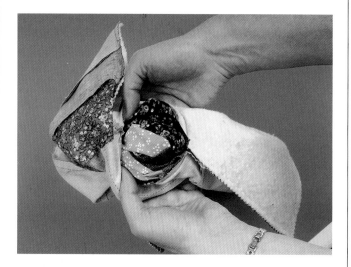

19. The corners of the placemat may not be square, so push them out gently with a pencil or crochet hook to make the corners square.

You want a nice, crisp point at each corner.

20. Press the placemat with the iron, taking care to fold in and press under the seam allowance at the opening.

21. Sew it closed with a blind stitch (see pages 26–27).

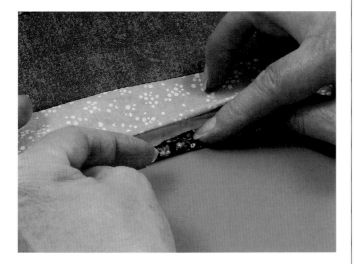

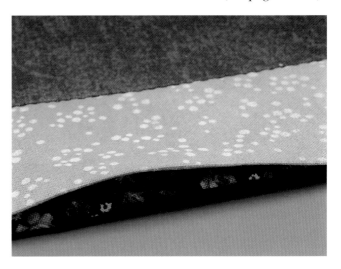

Hide the knot inside the seam to begin.

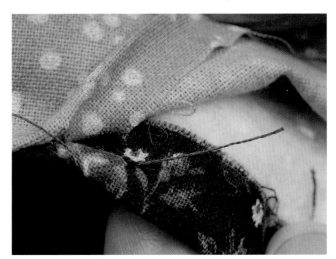

At the end of the seam, finish with a quilter's knot and bury it in the batting. Clip the thread.

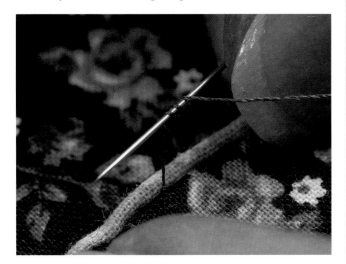

You want the edges of the seam to meet smoothly with no gaps.

Clip all threads close to the seam.

If you need to, press the placemat with an iron before going on to quilting it.

22. You are going to quilt the placemat by "stitching in the ditch" right beside the seams in the blocks.

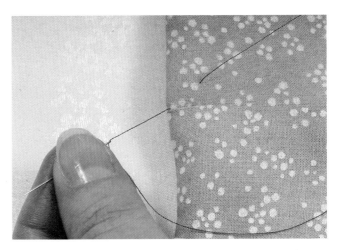

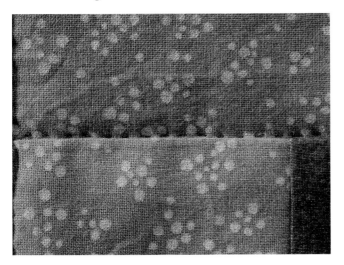

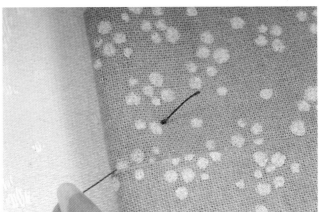

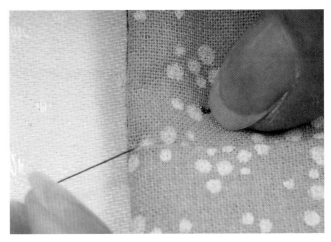

23. Use a neutral color quilting thread or one that matches the fabric. Bury the knot in the batting close to the seam where you want to begin quilting.

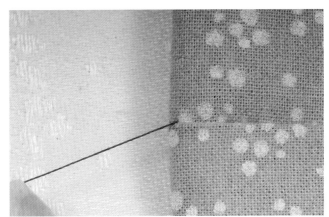

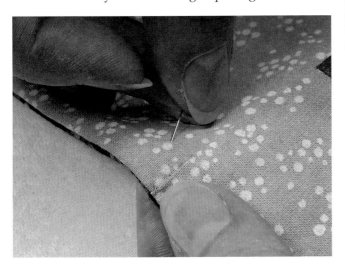

24. Begin stitching in the ditch using the stab stitch until you get beyond the thick seams at the edge of the placemat.

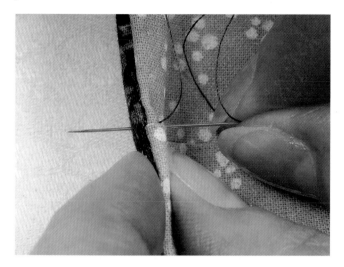

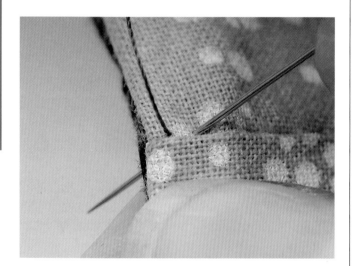

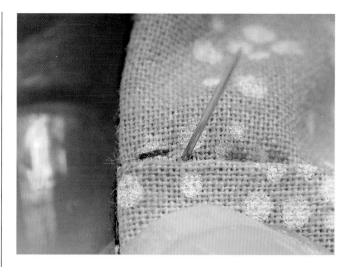

You can switch to the running stitch or rocking stitch to quilt most of the placemat. Be sure to catch the backing in each stitch. Try to keep the stitches the same size on the front and the back.

25. Finish quilting with a quilter's knot and bury it in the batting (see pages 17–18).

26. Stitch in the ditch next to every seam in the placemat, or you can just quilt around the darkest rectangles. The quilting keeps the batting in place through washing and daily use. How much quilting to do is up to you.

HOW TO MAKE THE OTHER PLACEMATS

1. Wash the fabric and trim off the selvages.

2. Make the template and cut out the fabric pieces for the block pattern.

Five-Bar: Use the rectangular template on page 73 (enlarged 200% on a photocopier) or make your own $2^1/4$ x 20-inch rectangle. It's easier to just cut a $2^1/4$-inch-wide strip on the cross grain of the fabric—making it as long as the fabric is wide. You need seven rectangles for each placemat. Use repeating colors as shown or choose another combination of colors for the five bars.

You might use one of the bar colors for the backing.

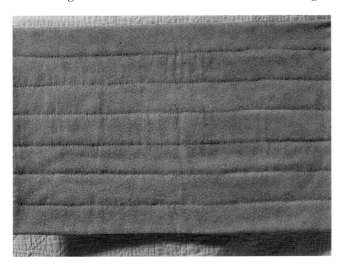

Nine-Patch: Use the square template on page 74 or cut your own $4^1/2$-inch square ($4^1/2$ inches on each side). You need eight squares of the darker fabric and seven squares of the lighter fabric for each placemat. Either color might be used as the backing.

Streaks of Lightning: Use the rectangular template on page 74 or cut your own $2^1/2$ x $4^1/2$-inch rectangle. You need fifteen rectangles of the flowered fabric and fifteen rectangles of the matching solid for each placemat. Either color can be used as the backing fabric.

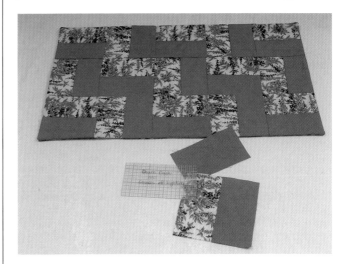

3. Assemble the pieces in the block pattern and pin them together carefully, so you can sew the correct pieces together. After each seam, put the piece back into the block to be sure it's right. Follow steps 11–21 for the Rail Fence placemat to complete the backing, batting, sewing, and turning steps.

4. Quilt by stitching in the ditch for the Five-Bar and Streaks of Lightning placemats. Of course, you may choose any quilt design, but this is what we did on the placemat.

The quilting shows on the back and makes a pleasing design on the fabric. Be sure to flip the mat over from time to time to make sure you are stitching in a straight line.

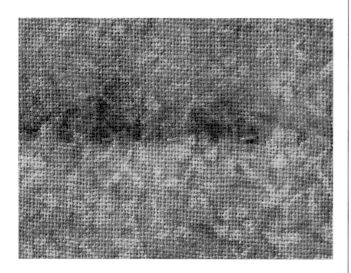

Quilt an X in each of the squares of the Christmas placemat. You will continue the quilting into the next square and on across the block. This is actually diamond quilting. See how the stitches disappear on the printed fabric, and how the stitches in the light squares add dimension and definition.

Quilting stitches are doing the work of holding all the layers smoothly in place, but they also are adding to the beauty of the overall design.

See how the stitches are all about the same size. This is what you are aiming for. You can also see that where the needle has gone through to the backing, those spaces between the stitches are about the same size as the stitches, too.

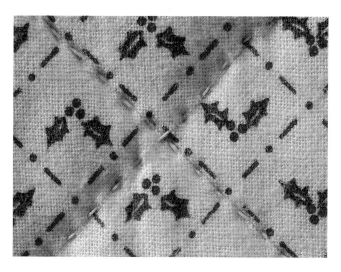

Close up you'll be able to see all your stitches, but no one else will be looking where you are looking. They'll just be admiring the creative work you have done.

7

Tote Bag Pocket

New Skills

- How to cut a template for a triangle
- How to cut a rectangular border to fit the quilt block
- How to sew a border
- How to attach a block to a bag
- How to finish edges with ribbon

Block Name: Friendship Star

Friendship Star templates

$2^1/_2$-inch square

$2^7/_8$-inch triangle (two $2^7/_8$-inch sides and one $4^1/_4$-inch side)

Draw a square that is $2^7/_8$ inches on all sides. Cut it in half on the diagonal. This is the right size triangle.

Border template

Rectangle, 2 inches wide and as long as the fabric. You will cut the border fabric to fit the block as you pin the border to it.

Makes two pockets.

Be sure to measure and cut carefully, or the block pattern will be crooked. This isn't too bad with a single block, but when you work on larger projects, it can throw the whole quilt out of line. You don't want to have to start over and take all the stitches out. (By the way, if you do have to remove stitches, it goes faster to cut every third stitch and pull the thread out.)

SHOPPING LIST
Tote Bag Pocket

Item & Quantity

☐ Fabrics, 4 fat quarters, light, dark, medium

☐ Fabric tote bag, 16-inch square

☐ Batting, thin- or medium-weight,
2 12-inch squares

☐ Thread, sewing and quilting
Colors to match the fabrics

☐ Needles, betweens and sharps 10, 11, or 12

☐ Brass safety pins, 1 package

☐ Pins, 1 package

☐ Template plastic, 1 8$^1/_2$ x 11-inch sheet

☐ Ribbon, to cover the handles (optional),
2 yards

☐ Scissors

☐ Clear ruler

☐ Mechanical pencil

☐ Thimble

☐ Iron

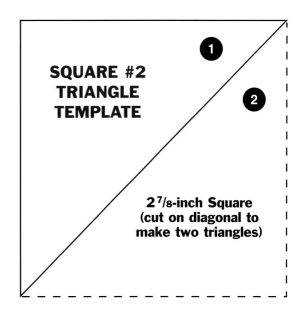

SQUARE #2 TRIANGLE TEMPLATE

2$^7/_8$-inch Square (cut on diagonal to make two triangles)

BORDER TEMPLATE

2 x 20-inch Rectangle

SQUARE #1 TEMPLATE

2$^1/_2$-inch Square

1. Choose your fabric. We used four different colors. We started with a large flowered fabric, found one with smaller flowers, and a solid for the quilt top. The backing is plaid with the same pinks and greens.

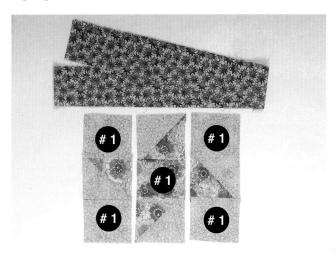

You could choose one of the fabrics you are using in the block to be the backing fabric, too. It's up to you. Remember to cut the backing larger than the finished block, when you get to that step.

2. Unfold the fabric and wash it. Dry on permanent press and iron out wrinkles before cutting. Also wash the tote bag so it will be softer and easier to stitch through.

3. Find the selvage and the straight grain of the fabric.
Cut the selvage off the fabric before you cut your pieces. It is too thick for you to sew through.

You will be cutting squares of two different sizes. You will cut out the larger square #2, and then you will cut the square in half to make two triangles. When you cut the triangles for this block, the diagonal side is going to be cut on the bias. This means the cut will be across the straight grain and the fabric will give or stretch along that edge. Hold it down with your hand as you cut.

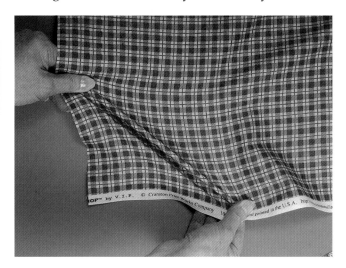

4. Trace the templates on page 89 or make your own using the same dimensions. Use the templates to cut the pieces of fabric for the quilt block:

- four green #1 squares
- one flowered #1 square
- two green #2 squares (four triangles)
- two flowered #2 squares (four triangles)

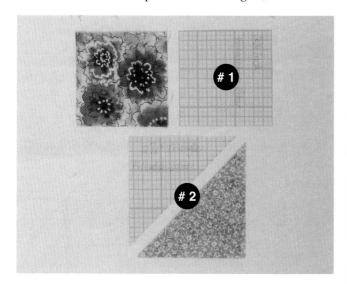

Cut each of the #2 squares diagonally into two triangles.

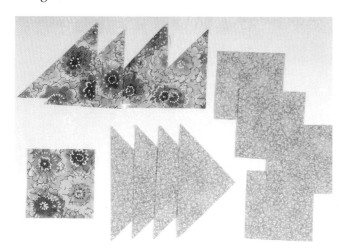

Lay out the pieces to be sure you have everything cut out.

5. Cut one long rectangular strip 2 inches wide to make the border that goes around the outside of the quilt block. You may need to cut several strips to complete the border, depending on how wide your fabric is. You can't cut the exact border length until you have finished the quilt block and can use it to measure.

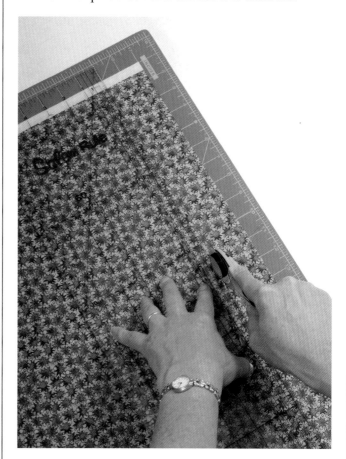

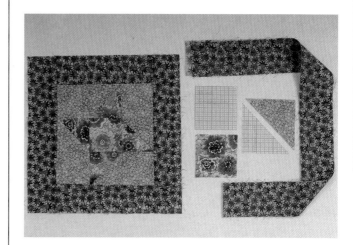

6. Lay the pieces out in the block pattern.

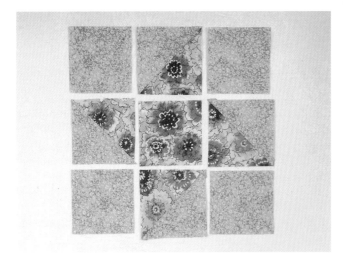

Mark a ¹/₄-inch seam line on the wrong side of each piece.

You will be sewing the triangles together to make squares. Pin the two pieces with right sides together.

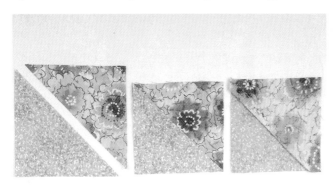

The right side of the fabric is the bright side; the colors are brighter, and the pattern, if there is one, is clearer.

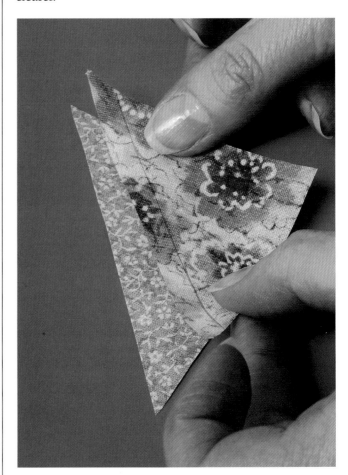

7. Sew along the seam line with a running stitch using regular sewing thread.

8. Check that you are stitching along the line on both pieces of fabric.

9. As you sew pieces together, put them back into the block to be sure you are sewing the right pieces together.

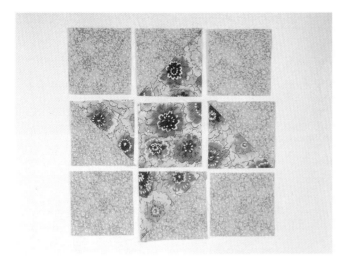

Now you will sew the squares together to make three vertical rows (A, B, and C). Press seams to the dark side. Lay each row back in the block to check the design.

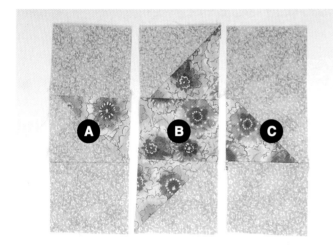

10. Sew row A to row B. Then sew row C to the other two. This will complete the quilt block. Press seams to the dark side.

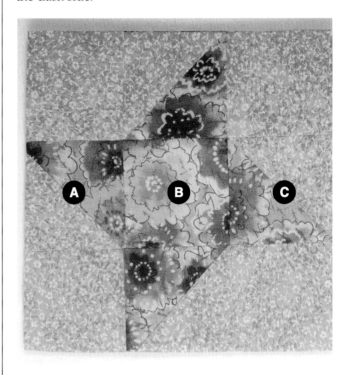

11. You will cut the border strip to fit around the four sides of the block.

Start by pinning the long border strip to one side of the quilt block. Be sure to pin them right sides together. Then cut off the extra border fabric that extends past the end of the quilt block. Sew the seam. Press the seam toward the border.

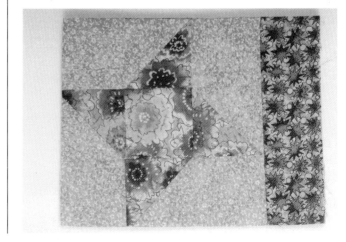

Pin the long border strip to the top of the quilt block and extend it past the first border. Cut off the excess. Sew the seam. Press it toward the border.

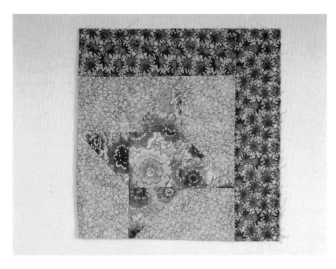

Cut another 2-inch border strip if you need it. Pin a border strip to the third side of the quilt block. Cut off the excess. Sew the seam. Press it toward the border.

Pin, cut, and sew the last border strip on the bottom of the block.

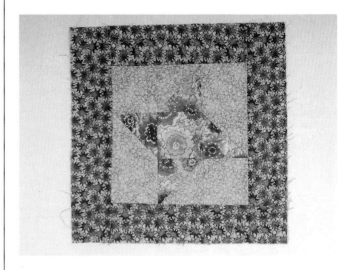

12. Press all the seams with an iron when you are finished sewing.

13. To cut the backing, lay the finished quilt block on the backing fabric. Cut around the quilt block, leaving an extra inch of backing fabric. Cut off the selvage, too.

Tote Bag Pocket

15. Layer batting, backing (right side up), and quilt top (wrong side up). The right sides of the backing and the block are facing each other.

16. Pin all three layers together with pins.

14. Now cut the batting using the backing as a template.

17. Mark a 3-inch opening with pins. Starting at one of the pins, sew around the outside edge of the block with a running stitch and a $1/4$-inch seam allowance (see pages 21–22). You might mark the seam line using a ruler and a pencil.

18. Trim the edges and turn the quilt block right-side out. Push out the corners with a pencil. Trim the excess batting and fabric at the 3-inch opening.

19. Press the quilt block, and press under the seam allowance at the opening.

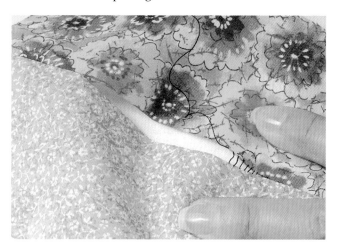

20. Sew the seam closed with a blind stitch (see pages 26–27). End the seam with a quilter's knot that you bury in the batting.

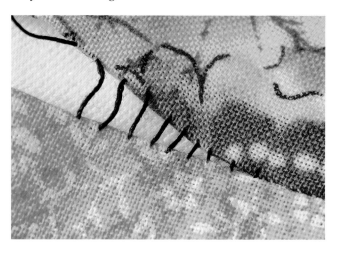

21. Using quilting thread, quilt the tote bag by stitching ¼ of an inch away from the seams of each piece in the block pattern.

See how the quilting echoes the shape of each piece in the block.

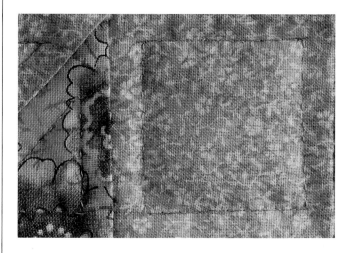

Quilt around the inside edge of the border next to the block.

Quilt only the top border ¹/₄ inch from the edge. Do not quilt the outer edge of the other three sides of the border because you will do that when you attach the block to the bag. The quilting will also be the stitching that attaches the pocket to the bag.

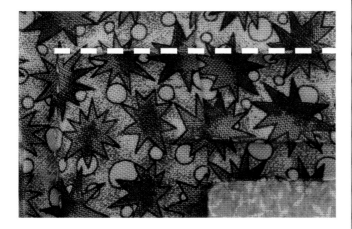

You may mark the seam line with a ruler and pencil ¹/₄ inch from the outside edge.

22. Pin the washed tote bag flat with safety pins.

23. Pin the ribbon onto the handles of the tote bag, leaving ¹/₂ inch of extra ribbon at both ends of the handles. These ends will be covered with the ribbon that goes around the top of bag.

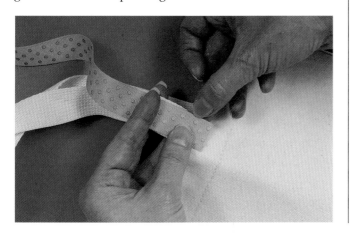

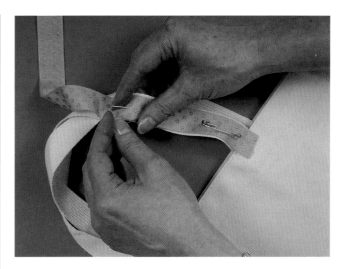

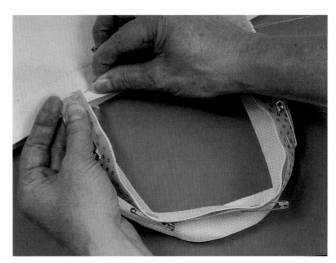

The ribbon is optional, but it gives you more practice with stiching and makes the bag prettier.

24. Stitch the ribbon to the handles with a running or stab stitch, depending on how stiff the fabric is.

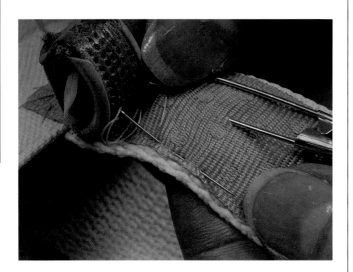

Then pin the ribbon around the top of the bag, covering the ends of the ribbon from the handles.

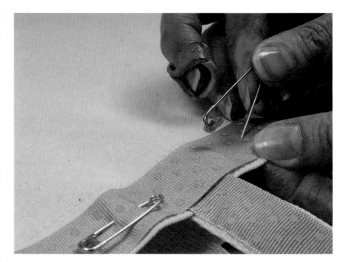

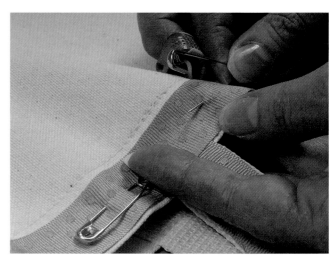

Sew the ribbon to the top of the bag, covering the ends of the ribbon on the handles.

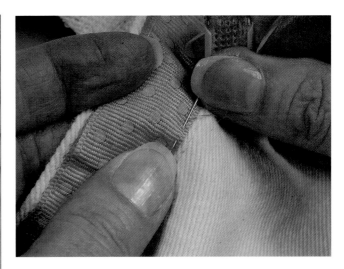

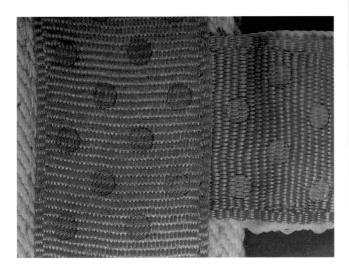

25. To neatly finish the ribbon, fold under the end, and sew the fold over the beginning of the ribbon. The ribbon will fray, so by turning it under, you get a nice finish and prevent the ends from unraveling.

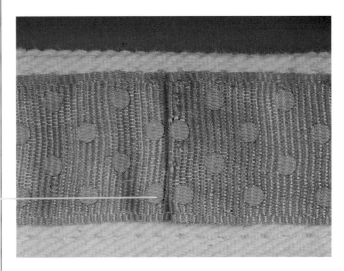

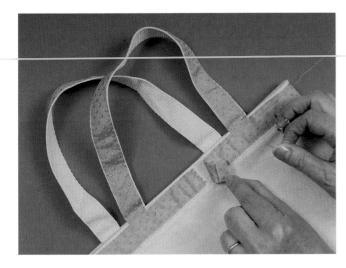

26. Find the center of the bag by measuring the width and length. Position the pocket in the middle or wherever you want it to be. Pin the quilt block on the tote bag, making sure you do not pin through the back of the bag.

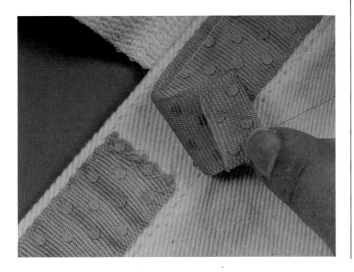

Use safety pins instead of long quilt pins so you are less likely to be stuck by a sharp point while you are sewing on the block.

Use lots of pints to hold the block in place.

27. Reaching inside the bag and putting the needle up through the top corner of the quilt block, begin to sew a ¹/₄-inch seam around the sides and bottom of the block with a stab stitch.

This part will be harder to sew because of the thickness of the bag and the fact that you have to work from inside the bag. Make a double backstitch loop at the beginning of the seam and another loop every inch or so to make the seam strong (see pages 21–22). Finish at the other top corner with a double backstitch loop—or two. The stitching will complete the quilting around three of the outer edges of the quilt block. Leave the top open for your pocket!

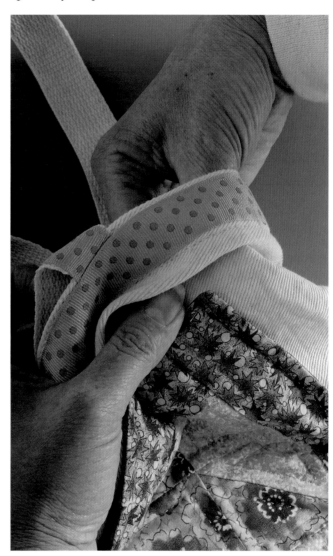

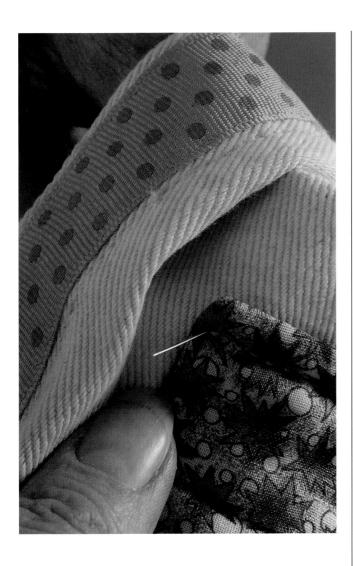

On the outside, the seam you sew to attach the pocket looks like $1/4$-inch quilting around the outside edge of the block. Try to keep your stitches even and about the same size as the other quilting stitches in the block.

This is the only sewing you will see on the inside of the bag. Small stitches will make the seam stronger.

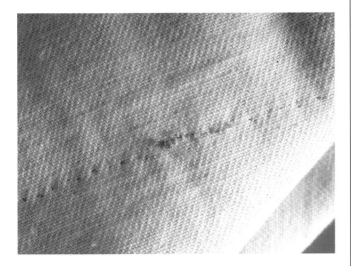

The final product is sturdy, useful, unique, and beautiful. You can use the leftover fabric to make a matching quilt pocket for the other side of this tote bag—or you can put it on another bag to give as a gift. By carrying a tote bag, you'll be helping the environment, too—you won't need paper or plastic bags to carry your shopping buys home.

8

Table Runner and Pillow Cover

New Skills

- One new quilt block
- How to make a table runner
- How to fussy cut a special block
- How to make sashing strips
- How to cut and sew long borders
- How to use a quilting template

Block Name: Shoo Fly

Fabric

Fabric for "fussy cut" middle square:
    fat quarter or 8 x 45 inches
Light/white fabric:
    22 x 45 inches
Dark/red fabric:
    40 x 45 inches (triangles, backing, sashing, and borders)

To use a different color fabric:
Sashings and borders:
    12 x 45 inches
    (subtract from red fabric)
Backing:
    16 x 45 inches
    (subtract from red fabric)

Shoo Fly templates

$4^1/_2$-inch square; $4^3/_4$-inch square makes two triangles. The two even sides are $4^3/_4$ inches, and the long side measures $6^3/_4$ inches.

Draw a square $4^3/_4$, and cut it in two on the diagonal to get two triangles of the correct size.

SHOPPING LIST
Table Runner and Pillow Cover

Item & Quantity
☐ Fabrics, see above
☐ Batting, thin- or medium-weight, 18 x 24 inches
☐ Thread, sewing and quilting Colors to match the fabrics
☐ Needles, betweens and sharps 10, 11, or 12
☐ Brass safety pins, 1 package
☐ Pins, 1 package
☐ Template plastic, 1 8½ x 11-inch sheet
☐ Quilting template, your choice
☐ Scissors
☐ Clear ruler
☐ Mechanical pencil
☐ Thimble
☐ Iron

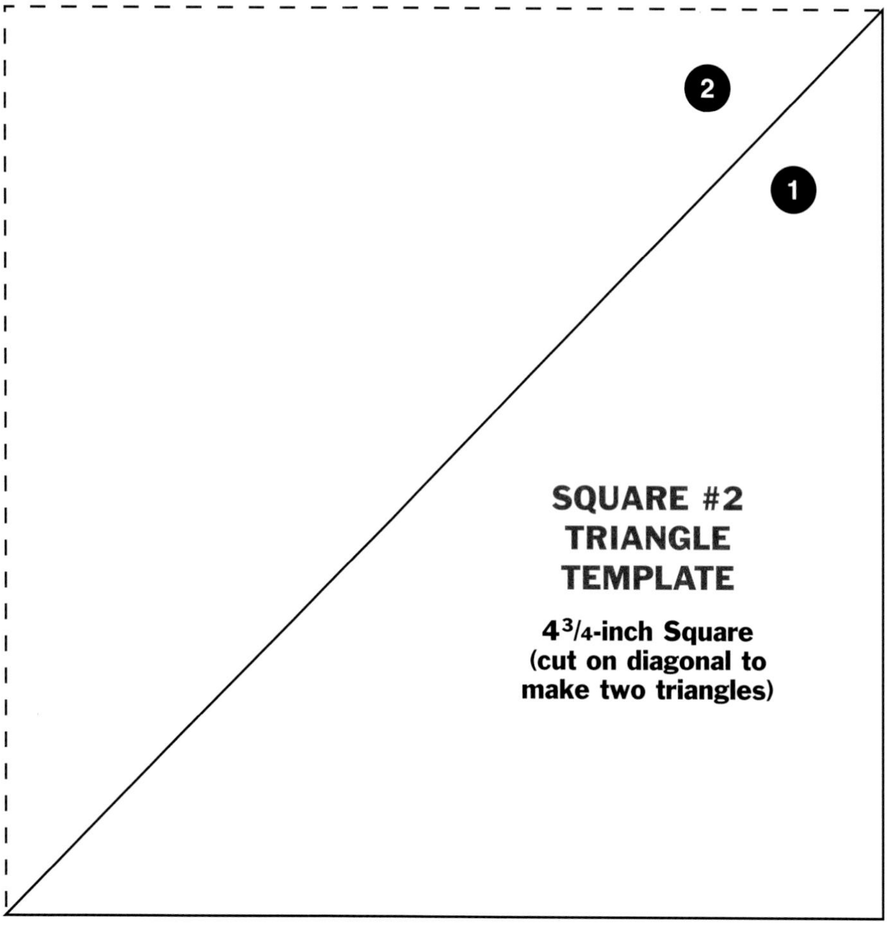
2
1
SQUARE #2
TRIANGLE
TEMPLATE
4 3/4-inch Square
(cut on diagonal to
make two triangles)

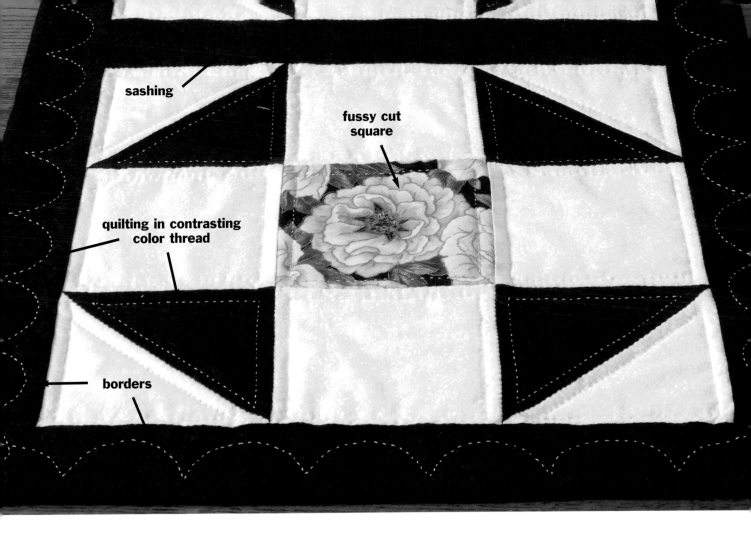

sashing

fussy cut
square

quilting in contrasting
color thread

borders

SQUARE #1
TEMPLATE

4½-inch Square

1. Choose your fabric. You need three or four different colors. We used a flowered fabric and two solid colors (white and red) to match the flowered fabric. We cut the same red fabric for the borders and the backing. You might chose to use the flowered fabric for the backing too. Check the fabric amounts on page 102 to adjust for this. It means that you will need 8 x 45 inches for the fussy cut squares plus 16 x 45 inches for the backing, or a total of 24 x 45 inches of the flowered fabric.

2. Unfold and wash the fabrics one at a time in cold water. Dry on permanent press and iron out wrinkles before cutting.

3. Make three templates for the table runner: one #2 square (two triangles), one rectangle, and one #1 square. You can see that there are four white squares and one flowered square in each block. The table runner has three quilt blocks in it, so you need to cut enough fabric pieces to make all three blocks.

While we show the triangle template—and many quilting books do— it is quicker and easier to cut a square and then cut it diagonally to get two triangles. This is a shortcut that many experienced quilters use. You can choose either way or experiment to see which works best for you and your fabric.

Always lay the cut pieces out in the block design to be sure you have everything you need before you start sewing. Lay out three complete blocks.

You will also need to cut 2$\frac{1}{2}$-inch wide strips that you will use for sashing pieces to go between the three blocks in the table runner and for the border pieces. Cut several long strips 2$\frac{1}{2}$ inches wide to begin. Measure 2$\frac{1}{2}$ inches and mark it along the length of the fabric. Connect the dots with a ruler and mark the cutting line.

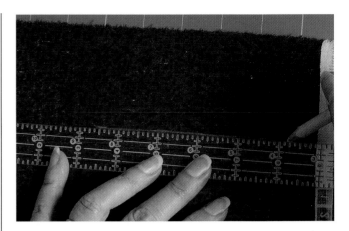

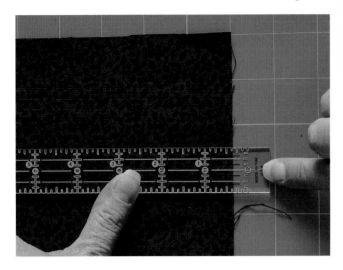

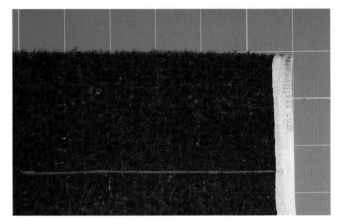

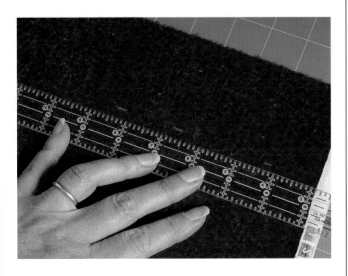

In all, you will be cutting these pieces for the table runner:

- three center #1 squares
- twelve white #1 squares
- six white #2 squares (twelve triangles)
- six red #2 squares (twelve triangles)

Later on, when the three borders are completed, you will cut

- four red sashing rectangles or strips (2$\frac{1}{2}$ inches wide)
- two long red border strips (2$\frac{1}{2}$ inches wide)

4. Now you will learn to "fussy cut" a flower for the center square of each block. To fussy cut, determine what you want to cut out, whether it is a flower, like the one in this runner, an animal, or a special design on the fabric. Place the clear plastic template over that special area on the right side of the fabric. Trace around the template with a mechanical pencil. Use sharp scissors to cut out the piece.

You will need three fussy cut squares.

5. Lay the pieces out in the pattern for each block.

6. Mark the stitching line ¹/₄ inch from the edge on the wrong side of the fabric.

7. Sew the pieces of each block together, beginning with the red and white triangles. Pin right sides together, and sew with a running stitch.

8. Press seams toward the dark fabric. With triangles, be careful not to stretch the fabric because it is cut on the bias. Only set the iron down—do not push it back and forth across the seam. Trim excess fabric from the edges of the new square, but don't cut the knots at the ends of the seam.

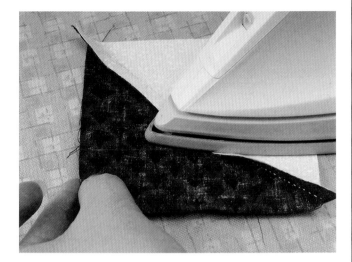

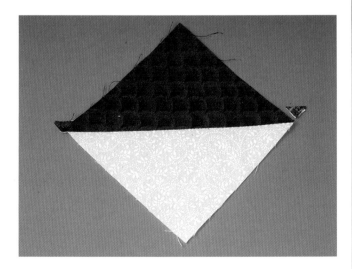

Lay the new squares back in the pattern.

9. Make a row by sewing the three squares across the top together. After each seam, lay the piece back in the design. Always pin the right sides of the pieces together. Then sew each of the three squares across the middle together. Next, sew the three squares across the bottom together. Press all seams toward the dark fabric. Lay the new rows back in the block.

109

10. Sew the top row to the middle row in the block. Sew this bigger piece to the bottom row to complete the block. Press all seams when you are finished. Repeat these steps for the other two blocks in the table runner.

11. The sashing has to fit the blocks you have sewn. Lay the sashing strip next to a finished block, measure and cut the length, and cut four sashing strips. If you need to, cut the selvage off first.

The sashing does not need to be any longer than the quilt block.

Lay the blocks and sashing down in order. You will have sashing, a block, sashing, the second block, sashing, and the third block. End with the last piece of sashing.

Start at either end. Pin a strip of sashing to the side of one block with right sides together.

Then pin and sew the second block to the other side of the sashing. Press seams toward the dark fabric.

Sew a new piece of sashing to the other side of the second block. Then sew the third block to that sashing. Sew the fourth piece of sashing to the end.

Sew with regular thread and a running stitch.

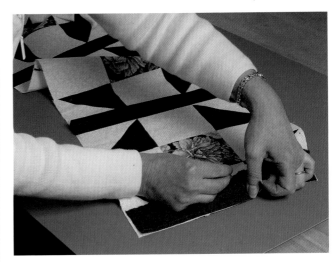

Press all seams.

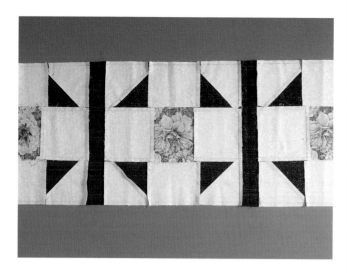

Now measure and cut a border piece $2^1/_2$ inches wide.

Lay the border strip along the top of the blocks. Cut off any excess border fabric.

Pin the border strip and table runner right sides together. Pin every 2 to 3 inches, because it is a long piece to sew.

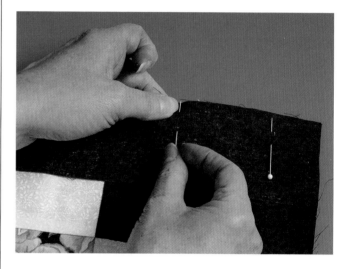

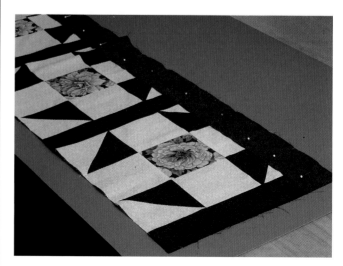

Pin the second border strip along the bottom of the runner with right sides together. You may need to cut another strip so it's long enough. Again, pin the pieces together every 2 to 3 inches. Cut off any excess fabric, and sew. Press all the seams toward the dark side.

12. Now you can cut the backing fabric using the pieced top as a template.

Then cut the batting using the backing as a template. This photo shows how to use the backing as a template. You may need to pin the backing to the babric if it slides around. Your table runner is much longer than the placemat in the photo.

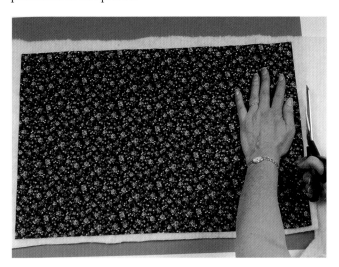

13. Mark the $1/4$-inch seam line on the wrong side of the fabric of the pieced top. Layer the three pieces of the quilt: batting first, backing (right side up), and pieced top (wrong side up). This photo from the placemat project reminds you how to stack the three parts of the quilt.

14. Pin the quilt together with safety pins. Sew around the outside with a running stitch and backstitch loops. Leave a 4-inch opening to turn the table runner right-side out. The larger opening is necessary because the table runner is a bigger quilt.

15. Trim the excess fabric. Turn the table runner right-side out. Push out the corners with a pencil. Trim the excess fabric and batting at the opening. Press under the seam allowances at the opening. Stitch closed with a blind stitch (see page 26–27). Press the table runner lightly with an iron. Do not press down on it.

16. Pin the three layers of the table runner together with safety pins to prevent the layers from shifting while you quilt. This is necessary because this project is so much larger than the other projects in this book. Place the safety pins every 3 or 4 inches all over the quilt.

17. You will be quilting in the white squares, the red and white triangles, the fussy cut squares, and along the borders. For most of these pieces, you will quilt 1/4 inch inside the seam line. Using the seam line as a guide may allow you to skip the step of marking your stitching line in pencil. If you need a stitching line, use pencil or nonpermanent marker on the right side of the fabric. You can buy a quilting template or make your own with the template plastic. We made up a flower template to use. Mark the quilting lines with a marker or pencil. We quilted flowers in the white squares and a garland design on the borders.

This is a quilting template that we purchased ready-made.

We used a white quilting pencil and white thread so it would show on the red fabric. Hold the template firmly so it doesn't shift around and mess up your quilting pattern.

18. Quilt the table runner with quilting thread by stitching 1/4 inch inside the seams of the pieces in each block. Quilt the flower designs in the white block and the garland design on the borders all the way around the runner.

You may have to overlap the arches in the design when you turn the corner to go down the next side.

Note how the quilting stitches provide definition and interesting texture to the table runner.

New Skills

- One new quilt block
- How to make a pillow cover
- How to layer the quilt a new way
- How to make a quilt block larger

Block Name: Churn Dash

FABRIC

- leftover from table runner or 4 fat eighths
- Muslin, $1/3$ yard 22-inch fabric
- 12 x 12 pillow form or 1 bag of stuffing

Churn Dash templates

The square and triangle templates used in the Shoo Fly block (pages 103–104) plus a rectangle $2^{1}/_2$ x $4^{1}/_2$ inches. (This template was also used for the Streaks of Lightning placemat, page 74.)

Makes one 12 x 12 inch pillow cover

With leftover fabric from the table runner, we can make a pillow cover.

The Churn Dash block uses two of the templates from the Shoo Fly block and the rectangle from the Streaks of Lightning placemat.

A pillow cover is a good use of little pieces of leftover fabric—one of the reasons for quilting in the first place!

1. Choose your fabric and cut these pieces:
- two white/light #2 squares (four triangles)
- two red/dark #2 squares (four triangles)
- one white/light #1 square
- four white/light rectangles
- four red/dark rectangles for the border (optional)

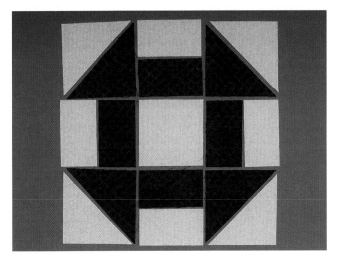

Lay the pieces out in the quilt block. Pin right sides together and sew the seams with regular thread using a running stitch. After each seam, lay the new piece back in the pattern. Press all seams.

You will notice that in the picture on page 116 the finished pillow cover has a red border around the quilt block. This was necessary because the pillow form we used was for a 16-inch square pillow. If you want to make a larger pillow cover, add a border—or two—following the steps for sewing the border on the tote bag pocket (pages 93–94). Lay the finished quilt block on the pillow form to see how wide the borders need to be. Careful measuring counts here. The finished block with borders should be $1/2$ to 1 inch larger than the front of the pillow.

117

2. You will need to quilt the pillow cover before sewing the backing on. Cut a piece of muslin or light fabric to use as the backing during quilting, using the block as a template. Cut batting to fit the backing. It is not necessary to find the right or wrong side, because the muslin will be on the inside of the finished pillow cover. This is a new way to layer the quilt: (1) the muslin backing, (2) the batting, and (3) the pieced block with the **right** side up, facing you.

3. Pin the three layers together with large brass safety pins. Now quilt the pieces in the block by stitching $1/4$ inch inside the seam lines. You do not have to bury the knots, because the muslin backing will be inside the pillow cover. The knots won't be seen.

4. When you have finished quilting the pillow top, use it as a template to cut the fabric that will be the back of the pillow cover. To sew the quilt top to the backing, you layer them in a new way. First, place the backing fabric on a tabletop with the right side facing up. Next, the quilted top goes right-side down onto the backing. The muslin with the knots in it is facing up. The right sides of the backing and the quilt top face each other.

5. Pin all the edges together. If you are using a pillow form, you will need to have a larger than usual opening in the seam, so you can get the pillow form inside it. If you're using stuffing, leave an opening large enough to put your hand in full of stuffing. Mark the opening with pins.

6. Sew the layers together, leaving the opening free. Trim the edges of the pillow cover.

7. Turn the pillow cover right-side out. Push the corners into shape with a pencil. Iron the cover and press under the seam allowance at the opening.

8. Insert the pillow form or fill the cover with stuffing. Pin the seam closed. Sew it closed with a blind stitch (see pages 26–27).

9. You can make pillow covers out of any of the quilt blocks in this book, by following steps 1–8.

Quilt Blocks

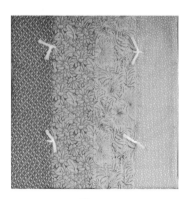

Bars

Rail Fence

9-Patch

Friendship Star

Shoo Fly

Resources

Smile Spinners
1975 Valley Road
Marysville, PA 17053
717-957-4225
www.smilespinners.com

WEB RESOURCES

www.aqsquilt.com
   The American Quilter's Society, Paducah, KY

www.calicocorneronline.com
   Quilt kits, fabrics, tips

www.fonsandporter.com
   Quilting fabric, supplies, blocks, information

www.kayewood.com
   Information, books, tools, patterns

www.memory.loc.gov/ammem/qlthtml/qlthome.html
   American Folklife Center of the Library of Congress
   Exploring America's diverse quilting traditions

www.quilttownusa.com/Town_Hall/experts.htm
   Quilting advice and explanations

www.smilespinners.com
   Quilting fabrics, supplies, information

TELEVISION
HGTV, Simply Quilts
Marianne Fons and Liz Porter: Sew Many Quilts

BOOKS

Beyer, Jinny. *Quilting by Hand*. Elmhurst, IL: Breckling Press, 2004.

Beyer, Jinny. *Hand Piecing with Jinny Beyer: A One-on-One Tutorial*. CD-rom. Elmhurst: IL: Breckling Press, 2005.

Chainey, Barbara. *Quilt It!: Quilting Ideas and Inspiration for Patchwork and Appliqué*. London, UK: David & Charles Publishers, 2001.

Fons, Marianne, and Liz Porter. *Quilter's Complete Guide*. Revised ed. Little Rock, AR: Leisure Arts, 2000.

Kaisand, Heidi, and Jennifer Keltner, eds. *Better Homes and Gardens Complete Guide to Quilting*. Des Moines, IA: Meredith Publishing Group, 2002.

Nelson, Suzanne, ed. *Fast, Fun and Fabulous Quilts*. Emmaus, PA: Rodale Press, 1996.

Pahl, Ellen, ed. *The Quilter's Ultimate Visual Guide*. Emmaus, PA: Rodale Press, 1997.

Pellman, Rachel Thomas. *Amish Wall Quilts*. Woodinville, WA: Martingale and Company, 2001.

Seely, Ann, and Joyce Stewart. *Color Magic for Quilters*. Emmaus, PA: Rodale Press, 1997.

Squire, Helen. *Show Me Helen*. Paducah, KY: American Quilter's Society, 1999.

Wickell, Janet. *The Classic American Quilt Collection: Stars*. Emmaus, PA: Rodale Press, 1997.